Venture Smith's Colonial Connecticut

A True Story of Freedom

Venture Smith

Elizabeth J. Normen

Illustrated by
Michael Borders

Connecticut Explored Inc.
P. O. Box 271561
West Hartford, CT 01627-1561
Ctexplored.org
ISBN   978-0-578-55062-6
For permissions contact publisher@ctexplored.org.
To purchase books visit venturesmithcolonialct.org.

ACKNOWLEDGEMENTS

I wish to thank curriculum consultant Carol Luckenbach for providing curriculum support. I also thank East Haddam town historian and Venture Smith authority Karl Stofko, Olivia White, Elizabeth Wood, Melanie Meehan, Aileen Novick, Lucianne Lavin, Daniel Broyld, Tammy Denease, and Nancy Steenburg for reading and commenting on early drafts. And many thanks to artist Michael Borders for his fresh interpretation of Venture Smith and his family in the illustrations he created especially for this book. — Elizabeth J. Normen

Design: John Alves

CONTENTS

MESSAGE TO TEACHERS   4

PART II: MEET VENTURE   5

Chapter 1:   Introduction   7
Chapter 2:   I was Born at Dukandarra   10
Chapter 3:   War Comes to My Home   14
Chapter 4:   Far From Home   16

PART II: VENTURE IN COLONIAL AMERICA   24

Chapter 5:   Venture Comes of Age   25
Chapter 6:   Venture Gets Married & Runs Away   28
Chapter 7:   A New Owner   30
Chapter 8:   Venture's Third Master Rents Him Out   39
Chapter 9:   Venture Buys His Freedom   44
Chapter 10:   Free at Last   47
Chapter 11:   Venture Purchases Meg's Freedom   50
Chapter 12:   100 Acres in Connecticut   53
Chapter 13:   Calling Out Cheats and Counting Blessings   56
Chapter 14:   Historians Fill in the Blanks   59

PART III: COLONIAL CONNECTICUT   64

Chapter 15:   Connecticut's Beginnings   65
Chapter 16:   Building a Puritan Colony   73
Chapter 17:   Growing Pains   79
Chapter 18:   The Colonial Economy   82

PART IV: SLAVERY IN COLONIAL CONNECTICUT   84

Chapter 19:   Slavery in Colonial Connecticut   85
Chapter 20:   Laws About Slavery   90
Chapter 21:   Slavery and the American Revolution   93
Chapter 22:   The End of Slavery in Connecticut   96
Chapter 23:   Why Venture's Story is Important   101

Glossary   104

Sources   106

MESSAGE TO TEACHERS

Connecticut's Social Studies Frameworks, adopted by the Connecticut State Department of Education in 2015, call for the study of Early United States History in grade 5. The frameworks "strongly suggest" using local and state history when teaching U.S. History at all grade levels (Frameworks, p. 5).

Venture Smith's Colonial Connecticut is based on a first-person primary source that supports student learning about colonial America and colonial Connecticut and provides students with an example of how state and local history is, as the frameworks state, a "window into larger national historical themes." It introduces students to issues of race and racism in the founding of the United States. It introduces students to the fact that slavery did not just happen in the South, and that New England, too, was founded on this cruel institution. This is important to understanding our nation's, and Connecticut's, founding.

And yet it is important for students to learn that the African American story is not only about slavery. Venture Smith's story is valuable in illustrating this: he begins and ends his life as a free person. Furthermore, students can learn from him about the life of a typical farmer/merchant/trader in the colonial period. His narrative tells us about the northeast coastal maritime economy encompassing Rhode Island, New York, and southeastern Connecticut.

Venture Smith's life story supports the grade 5 frameworks' emphasis on "analyzing and evaluating a variety of documents, sources, and perspectives" and the requirement that students consider the following questions (Frameworks, page 63):

- How do Americans define freedom and equality and how have American conceptions of freedom and equality changed over the course of U.S history

for members of various racial, ethnic, religious, and gender minority groups?
- Is America a land of political, economic, and social opportunity?
- What was the significance of Connecticut's contribution to America's story?
- Is the United States a "just" society and how has the concept of justice evolved over time?

This resource has several parts that provide teachers with flexibility. Parts I and II are Venture Smith's narrative, part III is a brief history of colonial Connecticut, including the Native Americans, and part IV discusses slavery in this state. You can begin with parts III and IV to provide context for Venture's arrival in the American colonies in the second half of the colonial period. Or, you can begin with Venture's own story in order to give students a sense of the challenges as lived by a real person in colonial America, especially for an enslaved—and, later, free—person of color.

Your students are likely new to reading non-fiction, history, and primary sources—especially a text written in 1798. They may need support to understand that this is not written in a novelistic style. It is compelling nonetheless because it is a true story of a real person's lived experience that reaches us across time.

This resource works in conjunction with its companion website, VentureSmithColonialCT.org, where educators will find more detailed curriculum connections, teacher guides, and curriculum materials and where students will find links to a primary-source library to support inquiry projects.

Venture Smith's Colonial Connecticut is designed to build on *Where I Live: Connecticut*, the social studies resource for grades 3 - 4, available at whereilivect.org.

PART I Meet Venture

A
NARRATIVE
OF THE
LIFE AND ADVENTURES
OF
VENTURE,

A NATIVE OF AFRICA:

But resident above sixty years in the United States of America.

RELATED BY HIMSELF.

New-London:
PRINTED BY C. HOLT, AT THE BEE-OFFICE.
1798.

Title page of Venture Smith's *Narrative*, published by *The Bee*, New London, 1798. East Haddam Historical Society

CHAPTER 1: INTRODUCTION

It had been a long and exhausting journey for the eight-year-old boy named Venture. The year was 1737. Venture had no idea where he was. He had no idea where his mother or his sisters and brothers were. He knew two things for sure. He knew he was far, far from home. And he knew his father was dead.

Over the last few months Venture had experienced many new and <u>traumatic</u> things. He had a new name. He had seen the sea for the first time and been on a ship. He was learning a new language. He had been on a long voyage, leaving his home in West Africa far behind.

The journey had taken more than three months. Many people had been very sick on the voyage. People often get seasick on boats, especially their first time. But the people had caught something worse: smallpox. Many had died. Their bodies had been thrown overboard. Venture had been lucky to survive, especially since his mother was not there to take care of him.

Such a journey would be overwhelming for anyone. How could he know what was ahead for him? But Venture was strong. He would later learn that the land under his feet was Rhode Island, one of the British colonies in North America. He would live in the colonies of New York and Connecticut, too, and be alive for the birth of the United States of America.

Venture's life story tells us a lot about colonial Connecticut, and so this is a book about colonial Connecticut. When Venture arrived, these colonies were already 100 years old. To understand the world Venture arrived in, read about the beginning of the Connecticut Colony in Part III.

To understand Venture's story, there's something important you should know about him.

Someone who arrives in a new country to live there is called an immigrant. Venture was from Africa, but he was not an immigrant.

Someone who leaves his homeland to escape war or violence is called a refugee. Venture left a home destroyed by war, but he was not a refugee.

Venture was a "spoil of war." An invading army had overtaken his village. The soldiers had murdered his father right before his eyes. He had been captured and separated from his family. His captors enslaved him. He was now the invaders' property. He could be bought and sold just like a cow or a coat.

The army had marched its captives to the coast. There he was sold to an American sailor. The sailor now decided what happened to Venture. The sailor decided to take the young boy to America.

In Venture's mind and in his heart, he was not a slave. Though it would take a very long time, he would make his way back to freedom.

We know Venture's story because he told it to someone who wrote it down and helped him get it published. *A Narrative of the Life and Adventures of Venture, A Native of Africa: but resident above sixty years in the United States of America. Related By Himself* was published in 1798. It is the earliest of five true Connecticut stories published by formerly enslaved people.

Venture tells us about the cruelty of slavery. Slavery did not just happen in the South. The Northern colonies had slavery, too. Venture tells us how one small boy grew up—against great odds—to become a successful landowner, farmer, and entrepreneur.

Venture will tell you his story, starting with his early childhood in West Africa. The words in **bold are Venture's own words**. Words that are not bold

Read my own words in BOLD...

are reworded so that the story is easier to follow. As much as possible, you will read **Venture's own words** as they were recorded and published in 1798.

Venture was an old man when he told his story. He was nearly blind. We don't know if the recorder changed any of Venture's words or changed his story, though the narrative says "nothing is added to what he related himself." We can only hope that his words were written down faithfully.

Learn more about colonial Connecticut in Part III and slavery in colonial Connecticut in Part IV.

About Venture

Venture did not know when he was born. He thought he was eight years old when he arrived in America. Scholars believe he was born around 1729.

Today we know it is generally disrespectful to refer to a person only by his or her first name. Enslaved people often were only allowed a first name. We do not know exactly when Venture added his last name "Smith." This book mostly refers to Venture Smith as "Venture." That is not out of disrespect. It is to make it easier for readers to follow the story.

CHAPTER 2: I WAS BORN AT DUKANDARRA

I was born at Dukandarra, in Guinea, about the year 1729. My father's name was Saungm Furro, Prince of the Tribe of Dukandarra.

1734

I was the eldest son in my family. My father named me Broteer. I had five brothers and sisters.

When I was about five years old, my parents had a disagreement. **My mother left her husband and country, and travelled away with her three children to the eastward.** She carried one of my siblings on her back and the other, a baby, in her arms. I walked beside her.

She didn't carry any food. **When we became hungry, my mother used to set us down on the ground, and gather some of the fruits which grew in that climate. At night we all lay down together in the most secure place we could find.** We heard the howls of wolves and lions, but our **Almighty protector** kept us safe.

We walked for two days and came to the edge of a great desert. After five more days of walking, we came to the end of this desert. We entered a beautiful country, and here my journey ended. My mother left me at the house of a very rich farmer and continued on her journey. She went on to the country where she was from.

The rich man's farm was in a wide valley through which a large river flowed. Every spring the river flooded, bringing fresh fertile soil to the

Where is Dukandarra?

Venture was from somewhere in West Africa. The area is now the country of Ghana. Dukandarra has not been found on maps of West Africa. Later in this story, he mentions Anamaboo. Anamaboo was a well-known slave-trading port in an area of West Africa known as the Gold Coast.

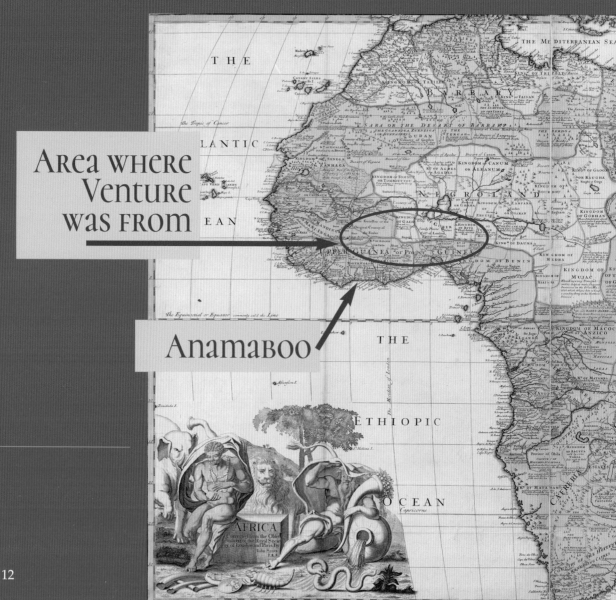

Area where Venture was from

Anamaboo

valley. After the floodwater drained away, the farmers planted their crops. The farmer whom I lived with had many acres of land. In addition to sheep, he had large herds of cattle and goats.

The farmer put me to work tending his flock of sheep. I worked with another boy. Every morning we drove the sheep between two and three miles to a pasture. At night we drove the flock back to the safety of the farm.

One day on the way home, a terrifying thing happened. Two large dogs ran out from a house and attacked me. Before the dogs' owner could pull them off, one dog bit my arm, and the other bit my thigh. The rich farmer was sent for, and he carried me home. I have scars to this day.

The rich farmer treated me kindly, almost like a son. I lived with him for about a year. One day my father sent a man and a horse to bring me home. The man paid the rich farmer for keeping me. When I got home my mother was there. She and my father were back together. They welcomed me home with great joy and affection. I was happy to be home again.

British map of Africa from around the time Venture Smith was born.
Library of Congress

13

CHAPTER 3: WAR COMES TO MY HOME

In this chapter, Venture tells of an invading army that attacked his village. We do not know who the invaders were or who had sent them. He says a "white nation" sent the invaders. We would not use that description today. He means a European nation. England, France, the Netherlands, Denmark, and Portugal were all active in trading for gold, slaves, and other goods in this part of Africa in the 1700s.

I had been home for only a few weeks when a messenger arrived. He had come from the place where the rich farmer lived. He had shocking news. A large army from a nearby nation had invaded. The army had weapons provided by **some white nation.** That nation had sent the invaders to take control of the rich farmer's country. The messenger said his **nation had made no preparation for war.** They had lived in peace for so long, **they could not defend themselves against this fierce enemy.** They were forced to flee.

The villagers **fled to the protection of a nearby chief but they were overrun there.** The messenger asked if my father would allow them to come and live under his rule. He agreed.

Just two days later, some soldiers **came to my father and informed him that the whole army was encamped** nearby. They said they would invade our village if my father did not **pay them a large sum of money, three hun-**

dred cattle, **and a great number of goats, sheep**, and other bounty. My father agreed to pay them, and the soldiers said they would not attack our village. But a short time later we heard they were going to attack us anyway.

My father decided we should flee for our safety. But the enemy discovered us in our hiding place when they saw the smoke from our cooking fire. My mother and my brothers and sisters hid with the other women and children in the tall reeds nearby.

My father and the men tried to defend us with their bows and arrows. I saw my father **from the reeds defending himself with great courage until he had to surrender himself into their hands.**

They then came to us in the reeds. A soldier hit me on the head with his gun and then grasped me round my neck. **I then had a rope put about my neck**. The soldiers tied up everyone hiding in the reeds, too. We were led to my father, who was bound with rope, too.

The soldiers then led us by the ropes to their camp. They made us watch as enemy soldiers beat and tortured my father, trying to force him to give up his money. **He thus died without informing his enemies of the place where his money lay. I saw him while he was thus tortured to death. The shocking scene is to this day fresh in my mind, and I have often been overcome while thinking of it**. He was a tall man with broad shoulders and great strength. He was kind, gentle, and a fair ruler.

CHAPTER 4: FAR FROM HOME

The army of the enemy was large. Immediately after they killed my father, we were **marched towards the sea, lying to the west. I was made** to wait on the leader of the scouting party. I had to carry water and his gun. At other times I had to carry supplies, cooking utensils, and a large flat stone used for grinding corn. Though I was pretty big for my age, I was still young, and these burdens were difficult for me to carry. But if I didn't do what I was told, I was punished.

As we were scouting we came across a herd of fat cattle.... These were immediately wrested from their keepers, and afterwards converted into food for the army. The enemy invaded village after village. They **had remarkable success in destroying the country wherever they went** and taking the villagers prisoners. I guessed that we walked **four hundred miles**.

When we arrived at **Anamaboo** on the coast, we were tired and almost out of food. The people there attacked us **and took enemy, prisoners, flock and all. I was then taken a second time. All of us were then put into the castle, and kept for market.**

A short time later I was put with other captives in a canoe. We were rowed out to a ship at anchor nearby. The ship's captain was James Collingwood of Rhode Island, and the first mate was Thomas Mumford. I was bought by Robinson Mumford, the ship's **steward, for four gallons of rum, and a piece of calico**

1739

Venture's Homeland

The place Venture calls Guinea is now the country of Ghana in West Africa. Descendants of Venture Smith visited Ghana in 2015 to learn about their family's history. Professor and poet Kwadwo Opoku-Agyemang from the University of Cape Coast spoke to the group. He talked about Ghana's history of slavery. It's a history, he said, that he feared his country had yet to heal from.

Source: "On Slavery's Doorstep in Ghana," *The New York Times*, January 30, 2015

The Trans-Atlantic Slave Trade

When Portuguese traders arrived on the west coast of Africa in the late 15th century, they found a well-established market for slaves in the Asante kingdom. But European demand for slaves in the 18th century caused a huge expansion of the slave trade. Slavery became more violent, and more enslaved people died in slave ships and by being forced to do hard labor under horrible conditions. Venture was caught up in this cross-Atlantic trade in humans.

Source: Bayo Holsey, *Routes of Remembrance: Refashioning the Slave Trade in Ghana*

The Middle Passage by Michael Borders

®MichaelBorders

cloth. He gave me the name **VENTURE** because he had purchased me as his own private investment or venture. In all, 260 captives were bought and became the ship's human cargo.

The ship sailed across the Atlantic Ocean to the island of Barbados. During the voyage, many of my fellow captives died of smallpox. When we arrived in **Barbadoes, not more than 200** of us were still **alive. These were all sold, except for myself and 3 more**, at the slave market there. We then sailed for Rhode Island.

When we arrived in Newport, Rhode Island, Mumford **sent me to live with one of his sisters** while he went on another voyage. Before that, he went away for a short time. He entrusted me with his trunks full of his belongings and with the keys to the trunks. He said I was not to give the keys to anyone, **not even to his father**. I promised to follow his instructions faithfully.

I arrived at his family's house, and sure enough, his father **asked me for his son's keys, as he wanted to see what his trunks contained. I told him** I could not do so. He insisted and threatened to punish me. But I did not give him the keys. I was afraid he would take them when I was not looking, so **I slung them around my neck, and in the day concealed them in my bosom, and at night I always lay with them under me**.

When Mumford returned, he asked for the keys. **I immediately took them off my neck and reached them out to him. He took them, stroked my hair, and commended me, saying in the presence of his father that his young Venture was so faithful that he never would have been able to have taken the keys from him but by violence.** He said he would not be afraid to trust his whole fortune to me because I had been raised by my parents to keep my word and to sacrifice my life to keep it.

I lived with Mumford's sister for about a year. I learned to speak English and to be a servant in the house. Mumford then took me to his farm on Fishers Island, New York before he went back to sea.

What is the Middle Passage?

Though Venture says he was put in a castle, it was probably a fort. Ruins of a fort built in 1759 can be seen today. Anomabu, in Ghana, was a major port for the slave trade in the mid-1700s. During the period of trans-Atlantic slave trading, it is estimated that nearly 500,000 enslaved people were shipped from Anomabu to America and the Caribbean. Nearly a quarter of them were children like Venture.

The voyage of enslaved people from Africa to the Americas is called the Middle Passage. Venture does not describe the horrors of the frightened people chained and packed closely in the hold of the ship without enough fresh air, food, or clean water. He only mentions his survival.

Points on the Triangle

Barbados was also a British colony. Large plantations there grew sugar cane and relied on thousands of enslaved Africans for labor. Most of Venture's fellow captives were sold there. They would not long survive the harsh conditions of plantation slavery.

Newport, Rhode Island was one of the largest slave-trading ports in the American colonies in the mid-1700s.

Workers in Colonial America

Self-employed worker
A person who worked for himself such as a farmer, merchant, or seamstress.

Indentured worker
A person who agreed to work for a period of time without pay in exchange for room and <u>board</u> or passage to a new country.

Apprentice
A person who agreed to work for a period of time without pay to learn a trade or skill. Parents apprenticed their children to learn a trade.

Slave or enslaved person
A person who was considered the property of an owner and forced by violence and law to work for life without pay.

Child laborer
A person who did the same kind of job grownups did. Children were considered workers just like adults.

Fisher island, 1882.
U.S. Coast and Geological Survey

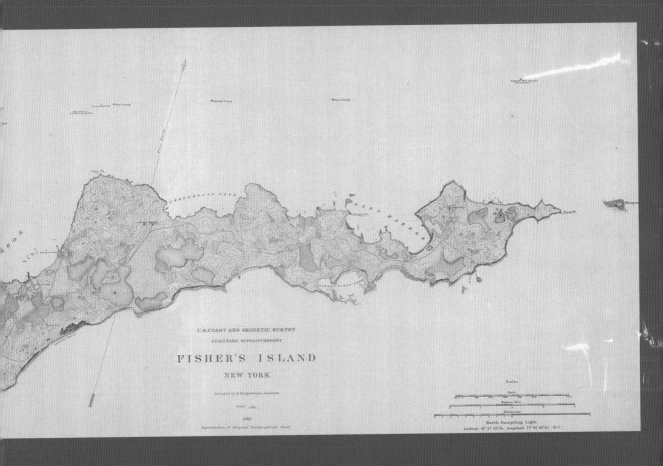

U.S. COAST AND GEODETIC SURVEY

J.E. HILGARD SUPERINTENDENT

FISHER'S ISLAND

NEW YORK

Surveyed by H. Bergenheim Assistant

Scale

1882

Reproduction of Original Topographical Sheet

North Dumpling Light.
Latitude 41° 17' 14".55, Longitude 72° 01' 16".67 (H.S.)

PART II Venture in Colonial America

CHAPTER 5: VENTURE COMES OF AGE

Beginning in 1740 when he was about eleven, Venture lived on the Mumford family's farm on Fishers Island. He was an orphan among strangers in a strange land. He spent the next fifteen years there and grew to be a man.

Sometime during Venture's first two years on Fishers Island, Robinson Mumford returned to sea and died. Venture then became the property of Robinson's father, Captain George Mumford. Venture does not mention this event.

The Mumford family was wealthy. From the early 1730s to the 1750s they leased Fishers Island from the Winthrop family. The Mumfords raised sheep for wool and to export to the West Indies. Venture was put to work carding wool. Carding was an important step in preparing sheeps' wool for spinning into yarn. It helps clean and detangle the wool fibers.

As you read, look for clues about what life was like on a large colonial farm, who did the work, and what other crops and animals were raised. There are clues about the work that enslaved people did on the farm and what happened if they didn't do it.

George Mumford died the year after he sold Venture. When Mumford died he owned more than twenty-five slaves.

Read my own words in BOLD...

The first of the time of living at my master's own place, I was pretty much employed in the house at carding wool and other household business. In this situation I continued for some years, after which my master put me to work out of doors.

After many proofs of my faithfulness and honesty, my master began to put great confidence in me. My behavior to him had been obedient. I then began to have hard tasks imposed on me. Some of these were to pound four bushels of ears of corn every night in a barrel for the poultry to eat. If I did not, I would be rigorously punished. At other seasons of the year I had to card wool until a very late hour.

1740

One day I got into trouble—the worst I'd been in since I came into this country. It happened because I served two masters. Sometimes when my master had gone from home in the morning and given me work to do that day, James Mumford, my master's son, would order me to do *this* and *that* business different from what my master directed me.

One day my master's son came up to me, big with authority, and commanded me very <u>arrogantly</u> to quit my present business and go directly about what he should order me. I replied to him that my master had given me so much to perform that day, and that I must therefore faithfully complete it in that time.

He then broke out into a great rage, snatched a pitchfork and went to lay me over the head with it; but I soon got another and defended myself with it, or otherwise he might have murdered me in his outrage.

He immediately called some people who were within hearing, and ordered them to take his hair rope and come and bind me with it. They all tried to bind me but in vain, tho' there were three assistants in number.

My upstart master then quit, put his pocket handkerchief before his eyes and went home with a design to tell his mother of the struggle with young Venture. He told her that their young Venture had become so stubborn that he could not control him, and asked her what he should do with him.

In the meantime I recovered my temper, voluntarily caused myself to be bound by the same men who tried in vain before, and carried before my young master, that he might do what he pleased with me. He took me to a gallows made for the purpose of hanging slaughtered cattle on, and suspended me on it. Afterwards he ordered one of his hands to go to the peach orchard and cut him three dozen of whips to punish me with. These were brought to him, and that was all that was done with them, as I was released and went to work after hanging on the gallows about an hour.

CHAPTER 6:
VENTURE GETS MARRIED AND RUNS AWAY

One of the cruelties of slavery is that marriage between enslaved people was not legal in most colonies, including in New York before 1809. Only people, not property, the colonies argued, could marry. But Venture says he "married Meg," who was also enslaved, around 1754. At the end of his book he writes that he is thankful that "Meg, the wife of my youth, whom I married for love, and bought with my money is still alive."

After I lived with my master 13 years, being then about 25 years old, I married Meg, a slave of his who was about my age.

My master had an indentured worker, **a certain Irishman, named Heddy, who about that time formed a plan of secretly leaving his master.** After he thought about it for a while, **he suggested it to me. At first I cast a deaf ear to it, and yelled at Heddy for harboring such a <u>rash</u>** plan. But the idea that I could gain my freedom by running away convinced me to join him. Heddy convinced two of my fellow slaves to accompany us.

We made plans, collecting **out of our master's** storage room **six great old cheeses, butter, and one whole batch of new bread. When we had gathered all our own clothes and some more, we took them all about midnight, and went to the waterside. We stole our master's boat, embarked, and then directed our course for the Mississippi River.**

We promised not to **betray or desert one another on pain of death. We first steered our course for Montauk Point on the east end of Long Island. After our arrival there we landed and Heddy and I** went in search of fresh water. He returned to our companions who were cooking a meal. I continued looking for water. **I returned to my fellows not long after. They informed me that our clothes were stolen** out of the boat but didn't know who was the thief. **They suspected Heddy as he was missing.** I yelled at the two fellows **for not taking care of our things** and sent them in search of Heddy. They **overtook him in Southampton and returned him to the boat.** I then thought I might be rewarded for returning him to my master. We returned to Fishers Island. **I informed my master that Heddy was the ringleader of our revolt, and that he had used us ill. He immediately put Heddy into <u>custody</u>, and myself and companions were well received and went to work as usual. Not a long time passed after that before Heddy was sent by my master to New London's jail.**

At the close of that year I was sold to a Thomas Stanton, and had to be separated from my wife and one daughter Hannah, who was about one month old. He resided at Stonington Point.

Advertising for Runaways

George Mumford placed a notice on April 1, 1754 in at least one newspaper advertising for the return of "Four men servants, a white man and three [black men], who hath taken a large two-mast boat, … and a large white pine canoe…" He identified them as Joseph Heday, Fortune, Venture, and Isaac. Fortune and Isaac were also enslaved. Mumford offered "20 pounds New-York currency reward and all reasonable charges paid" for their return.

Primary Source

See the ad at Runaway Connecticut, a project of Wesleyan University
wesomeka.wesleyan.edu/runawayct/items/show/5482

CHAPTER 7: A NEW OWNER

In late 1754 George Mumford sold Venture to Thomas Stanton II. Stanton's great-grandfather was a founder of Stonington, Connecticut and a friend of the Mohegan sachem Uncas. Thomas Stanton was in business trading goods between Connecticut and the West Indies. His son Daniel moved to Barbados to further the family business there.

Venture now lived in Stonington. He was separated from his wife, Meg, and baby daughter, Hannah. They were still enslaved by Mumford on Fishers Island.

In late spring 1756 Venture was reunited with Meg when Stanton bought her. Hannah, a toddler, was left behind. She remained enslaved to Mumford. Slave owners did not care about separating a mother and father from their children.

Venture had already begun to earn and save money from work other people paid him to do apart from his work for Stanton. He tells us important information about how the colonial economy worked. For example, he had coins of various kinds. The British pound was the official currency. But British money was scarce. There were no banks in the colonies. Instead, people accepted and used all kinds of coins, including Spanish, Portuguese, French, and English coins. A coin's value was based on how much precious metal, such as gold, silver, or copper, it contained.

Paper money was issued by each colony, but people didn't trust its value. People also gave each other written agreements—called notes—that said that *the person owed a certain amount of money to the other person. Today when people need to borrow money to make a large purchase, they usually get a loan from a bank. In colonial America people borrowed money from each other.*

Venture also bought and sold in different currencies. Sometimes he used pounds. Sometimes he used Spanish dollars, lawful money, or old tenor. It shows how complicated buying and selling was in the colonial economy.

Venture was quick to learn how the colonial economy worked and—even as an enslaved person—how it could work for him. Soon after he was bought by Stanton he loaned his savings to Stanton's brother Robert. But Venture was not always treated honestly and honorably, as you'll find out.

To this place I brought with me from my late master's two Johannes, three old Spanish dollars, and two thousand of coppers, besides five pounds of my wife's money. This money I got by cleaning gentlemen's shoes and boots, by catching musk-rats and minks, raising potatoes and carrots, etc. and by fishing in the night and at odd spells. All this money amounting to near 21 pounds York <u>currency</u> my master's brother, Robert Stanton, borrowed from me, for which he gave me his note.

1756

About one year and a half after that time, my master purchased my wife, pregnant with our second **child, for 700 pounds old tenor.** This child, named Solomon, was born later that year.

One time my master sent me two miles after a barrel of molasses, and ordered me to carry it on my shoulders. I made out to carry it all the way to my master's house.

In 1758 our son Cuff was born.

Meg and I had lived with Stanton for about four years when I had **a falling out with my mistress, the master's wife.**

My master was gone to Long-Island hunting. **At first the quarrel began**

What was in Venture's wallet?

When Venture says he bought or paid for something in dollars, he means Spanish dollars. Johannes were Portuguese coins. The colonies used the British pound until 1792.

Old tenor was paper currency issued by the Connecticut Colony in 1709. Lawful money is another term for paper money issued in the colonies.

While British pounds, shillings, and pence were rare in the colonies, British half pence and farthings (quarter pence) made of copper were available. These may have been the "coppers" that Venture had.

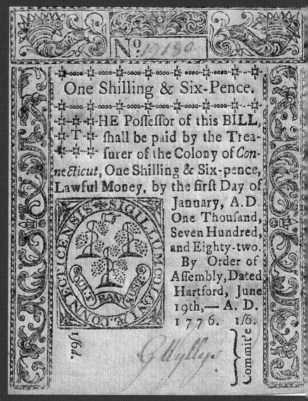

Paper currency issued by Connecticut in 1776.

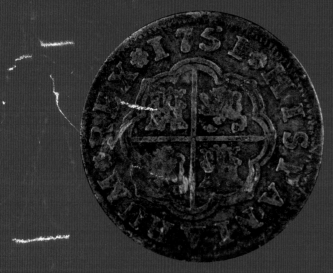

A Spanish dollar

Instead of dollars and cents...

	Symbol	Equivalent
Pound	£	
Shilling	s	20 shillings = 1 pound
Pence	d	12 pence = 1 shilling

Ways to Buy and Sell in Colonial America

Barter	Trade goods you own or your labor for something someone else owns that you want. You could sometimes arrange to deliver your goods later, such as when your crops were ready to harvest.
Book credit	Shopkeepers would keep track of how much you bought in a book called a ledger. When you had goods he wanted to sell in his shop, he'd buy them from you and credit your account for the value.
Bills of exchange	You could give an "I Owe You" to the person you bought something from. That person could use that to buy something from someone else. Then you would owe the money to that other person.
Coins and paper money	Coins were the most dependable currency. Paper money could become worth less over time. This means someone might give you less than 1 pound's worth of goods if you paid with a colonial old or new tenor bill.

between my wife and her mistress. I was then at work in the barn, and hearing a racket in the house, I ran to see what had broken out. When I entered the house, I found my mistress beating my wife over nothing, a mere <u>trifle</u>. I asked **Meg to beg pardon of her mistress for the sake of peace.** But my mistress turned her blows on me. **She took down her horse-whip, and while she was glutting her fury with it, I reached out my great black hand, raised it up and received the blows of the whip on it which were designed for my head.** I grabbed the whip and threw it in the fire.

1759

When my master returned, his wife told him what happened, but he didn't do anything, and he **mentioned not a word about it to me. Some days after his return, in the morning as I was putting on a log in the fireplace, not suspecting harm from any one, I received the most violent stroke on the crown of my head with a club two feet long and as large round as a chair-post. This blow very badly wounded my head, and the scar of it remains to this day.**

The first blow made me have my wits about me, for as soon as he went to hit me again, **I snatched the club out of his hands and dragged him out of the door. He then sent for his brother to come and assist him, but I** grabbed **the club he wounded me with, carried it to a neighboring Justice of the Peace, and complained of my master. He advised me to return to my master, and if he abused me again,** to report him. I agreed, **but before I set out for my master's,** my master and his brother Robert came **after me. The Justice cautioned my master. He asked him** the reason he treated me so **unjustly, and told him what the consequence would be if he continued the same treatment towards me.**

We left, my master riding his horse in front of me and his brother, also on horseback, behind me. Down the road out of sight, they got off their horses and fell **to beating me with great violence. I became enraged at this and immediately turned them both under me, laid one of them across the other, and stamped both with my feet.**

A short time after this I was taken by a constable and two men. They carried me to a blacksmith's shop and had me hand-cuffed. When I returned home my mistress was relieved to see me so. I showed her my hand-cuffs, and gave her thanks for my gold rings. For this my master commanded a fellow slave to fetch him a large ox chain. This my master locked on my legs with two padlocks.

I continued to wear the chain peaceably for two or three days, when my master asked me whether I had not better be freed from my chains and go to work.

I answered him, "No."

"Well then," he said, "I will send you to the West Indies or banish you, for I am resolved not to keep you."

I answered him, "I crossed the waters to come here, and I am willing to cross them to return."

For a day or two after this not anyone said much to me, until one Hempsted Miner, of Stonington, asked me if I would live with him.

I answered him that I would.

Miner asked me to be difficult and uncooperative so that he could buy me for a bargain price. In return he said he'd give me a good chance to gain my freedom when I came to live with him.

I did as he requested of me. Not long after Hempsted Miner purchased me for 56 pounds lawful money. He took the chain and padlocks off me immediately.

In the fray between my master Stanton and myself, he broke open my chest containing his brother's note to me and destroyed it.

Who was Hempsted Miner?

Hempsted Miner lived in Stonington. He appears to not have been very successful. He was the grandson of Joshua Hempsted of New London, who died in 1758. Joshua Hempsted's house is now a museum where you can learn about the life of another enslaved person, Adam Jackson.

Visit ctlandmarks.org/hempsted

A recreation of the attic space where Adam Jackson, an enslaved man owned by Joshua Hempsted, may have slept in the Hempsted House in New London. Hempsted lived from 1678 to 1758. He kept a diary from 1711 to 1758. He recorded purchasing Jackson in 1727. Jackson was enslaved for more than 30 years. He became free in 1760 and died in 1764.

Robert Stanton, A Slave Owner, Too

Just a few years after this episode, on June 13, 1760, Robert Stanton advertised in the *New London Summary* for the return of Caesar, who had run away from him. Caesar was twenty-five years old.

See the ad at wesomeka.wesleyan.edu/runawayct/items/show/5389

Robert Stanton House, Stonington. Library of Congress

CHAPTER 8: VENTURE'S THIRD MASTER RENTS HIM OUT

The violent incident between Venture and the Stantons led to Venture's sale. Thomas Stanton had put Venture in chains to get him under his control again. A man in chains, however, is not doing any work. Stanton needed Venture to work. He tried to get Venture to obey him by threatening to sell him in the West Indies. Venture had seen Stanton use extreme violence against him. He also saw that the local Justice of the Peace was reluctant to help him. He had a wife and children to think about, too. But he did not give in. Instead, he agreed to be sold to Hempsted Miner.

In 1759 Venture was again separated from his wife and children. He was now thirty years old, his daughter Hannah was five years old (and still enslaved to the Mumford family), his son Solomon was three, and his son Cuff was just a year old. Miner promised Venture a path to freedom, but he would not keep his word. Venture was, however, given some say in who bought him next, and this would help get him back on the path to freedom.

But first his life took a detour to Hartford. For the first time since he arrived in the colonies, Venture was a house servant. Daniel Edwards was a lawyer and judge. Venture lived with Edwards for about a year.

Immediately after my present master bought me, he determined to sell me at Hartford. As soon as I learned of it, I thought I had better secure the small amount of money I still had in a better way than loaning it to

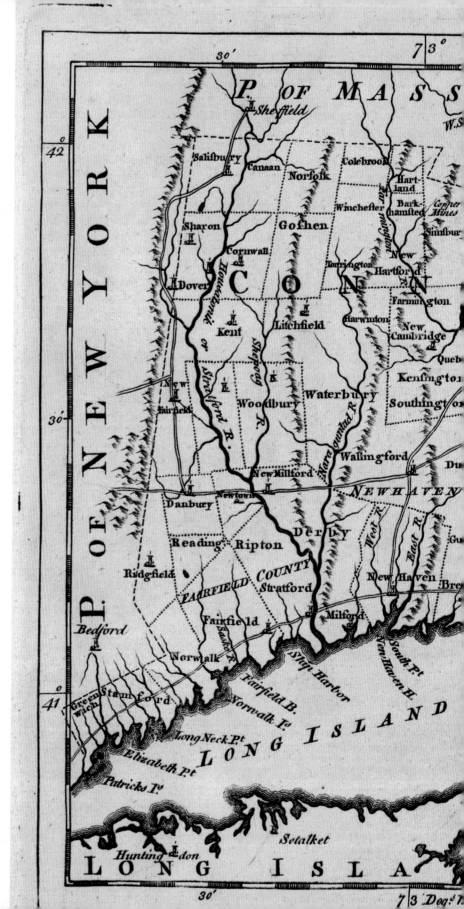

Connecticut and
Rhode Island
colonies, 1758.
Library of Congress

30'   7 2°   30'

° 42

MA**CHUSETS BAY PROVINCE**

E. Springfield

Sutton

Duglass

Wrentham

Bellingham

Union

Woodstock

Smith-field

Smith R.

Little R.

Skantik R.

Willing-ton

Ashford

Killings-ley

Paskow R.

Glocester

Rehoboth

CTICUT

E. Windsor

Coventry

Willimantic R.

Pomfret

PROVIDENCE

RHODE

Barrington

Bolton

Windham

Mortlake

Scituate

Pottuxet R.

Warwick

Bristol

Tiverton

Hebron

Hope R.

Canterbury

Coventry

Float R.

Bristol

Hasenbury

Butlers I.

Lebanon

Beaver R.

Little R.

Volun-town

West Greenwich

Greenwich North

NARR Hope I.

Prudence I.

RHODE ISLAND

Portsmouth

Middleton

Fox-land

Little Compton

30'

Colchester

Plain-field

Preston

Kingston

Tower Hill

Newport

Norwich

Falls

Exeter

Richmond

ISLAND

3 Miles I.

Hadham East

NEW LONDON COUNTY

Thames R.

Shawas R.

Woods R.

Westerley

Piekatuk R.

South Kingston

Judeth Pt & Rocks

Thale Rock

Brentons Pt.

Seakonnet Pt.

Deep R.

Lime

N. London

Groton

Stoning-ton

Pauls R.

Seabrook

Nahautik B.

Black Pt.

Watch Pt.

Quankorugok Pt.

Vinigret Pt.

Connecticut R.

Pipestaves Pt.

Fishers I.

Block I.

Duck I.

Plumb I.

° 41

Shelter I.

Gardners I.

British Miles

5   10   15   20

Montuck Pt.

A MAP of the COLONIES of CONNECTICUT and RHODE ISLAND, Divided into Counties & Townships; from the best Authorities By Tho Kitchin Geog.

41

Stanton. I buried it in the earth a little distance from Thomas Stanton's, in the road over which he passed daily.

A short time after my master carried me to Hartford, and first proposed to sell me to one William Hooker of that place.

Hooker asked whether I would go to German Flats (New York) with him.

I answered, "No."

He said he'd take me by force if he had to. He said, "I will tie you down in my sleigh."

I replied to him that if he carried me in that manner, no person would purchase me, for it would be thought that he had a murderer for sale. After this he tried no more, and said he would not have me as a gift.

My master next offered me to Daniel Edwards, Esq. of Hartford, for sale. But he did not buy me. Instead, my master rented me to him for ten pounds, and returned to Stonington.

Mr. Edwards tested my honesty, and, after being satisfied, placed considerable trust and confidence in me. He put me to serve as his cup-bearer and waiter. When there was company at his house, he would send me into his cellar and other parts of his house to fetch wine and other things for him.

When I had been with him some time, he asked me why my master wished to part with such an honest man, and why he did not keep me for himself. I replied that I could not give him the reason, unless it was to convert me into cash, and speculate with me as with other commodities. I hope that he can never justly say it was on account of my ill conduct that he did not keep me himself.

Mr. Edwards told me that he would be very willing to keep me himself, if it was not unreasonable and inconvenient for me to be parted from my wife and children. He said he would furnish me with a horse to return to Stonington, if I wanted to go.

As Miner did not appear to be calling for my return to Stonington any time soon, I went, and called at my old master Stanton's first to see my wife, who was then owned by him. My old master appeared much ruffled at my being there. I left my wife before I had spent much time with her, and went to Colonel Oliver Smith's. Miner had not paid Stanton all he owed him and instead had given Col. Smith a bill of sale of me. Oliver Smith paid the bill of sale and became my new owner. This was the third time of my being sold, and I was then 31 years old.

1760

CHAPTER 9: VENTURE BUYS HIS FREEDOM

Oliver Smith was ten years younger than Venture. He was in his twenties when he owned Venture. He later fought in the American Revolution and became a colonel in 1777. Venture and the Smith family would have a long association.

Private land ownership was unknown in the African societies where Venture came from. Venture came to understand the ways of New England, and that owning land meant independence. He continued to earn money to buy his freedom. As you read, look for more clues about the many ways someone could earn money in the colonial era.

Venture says that around 1760, with money he had earned, he "laid out in land" adjoining Thomas Stanton's land. Venture may have rented the land. In 1770 he bought land from John and Eunice Denison. The land is now part of the State of Connecticut Barn Island State Preserve.

Miner had broken his promise to allow me to buy my freedom. I was now very anxious to do so. **I asked my master (Oliver Smith) one time if he would consent to have me purchase my freedom. He replied that he would. I was then very happy, knowing that I was at that time able to pay part of the purchase money by means of the money which I had buried. This I took out of the earth and** gave **to my master** with the understanding that I would earn interest on it until the sale was completed. I had a friend, a free black man, hold the note to keep it safe for me.

What I still owed, **my master agreed to wait for, until I could** earn enough to pay him. **I still continued to work for Col. Smith.**

The interest I received on my note **and with some** money **I got by fishing, I laid out in land adjoining my old master Stanton's. By cultivating this land at times when my master did not require my labor, in two years I** saved up ten pounds. I invested this money with my master, too, and my friend held my note for safekeeping.

1762

Being encouraged by the success which I had met toward purchasing my freedom, I again asked **my master for a further chance** to earn money. I asked if I could go out to work that winter. **He agreed to this on condition that I would give him one quarter of my earnings. On these terms I worked the following winter and earned 4 pounds 16 shillings. One quarter** of it went to my master for the privilege of working elsewhere that winter, **and the rest was paid him** toward purchasing my freedom. This, added to the other payments, made up 44 pounds, 8 shillings. I was then about thirty-five years old.

The next summer I again desired he would give me a chance of going out to work. But he refused and answered that he must have my labor this summer, as he did not have it the past winter.

I replied that I considered it as hard that I could not have a chance to **work** for someone else to earn money during the best season.

He asked me what I would give him for the privilege per month. I replied that I would leave it to **his own generosity to determine what I should** pay him per month of my earnings.

"Well then," said he, **"two pounds a month."**

I answered him that if that was the least he would take I would be contented.

Accordingly I hired myself out at Fishers Island, and earned 20 pounds. Thirteen pounds six shillings my master got for letting me work for someone else instead of for him, and the rest I paid him for my freedom. This made 51 pounds 2 shillings which I had paid him.

In October I went and worked for six months on Long Island. In that six month's time I cut and corded 400 cords of wood, besides threshing out 75 bushels of grain, and received my wages. During that time, I only bought one pair of shoes. At night I lay on the hearth, with one coverlet over and another under me. I returned to my master and gave him what I received of my six months labor. This left only 13 pounds 18 shillings to make up the full sum for my freedom.

My master liberated me, saying that I might pay what was left if it was convenient, otherwise it would be all right to not pay him. The amount of money which I had paid my master towards my freedom was 71 pounds 2 shillings. The reason my master gave for asking such an unreasonable price was, he said, to use in case the town ever made him take care of me.

Being 36 years old, I left Col. Smith once for all. I had already been sold three different times, made considerable money with seemingly nothing to show for it, been cheated out of a large sum of money, lost much by misfortune, and paid an enormous sum for my freedom.

1765

CHAPTER 10: FREE AT LAST

In 1765 Venture finally was a free man through his own sweat and hard work.
His wife and three children were still enslaved. He now set his sights on
earning the money to buy his family's freedom. He moved to Long Island,
New York.

Venture worked at cutting wood. Wood was a valuable product in the
colonies. It was an important building material, and was used as fuel for heat
and cooking. It was also used in making barrels. Barrels were the main way
that products were packed for shipping. Venture found that cutting and selling
wood was a good way to make money.

Venture purchased his two sons and then hired the oldest one out. It was
common in the colonies for parents to indenture their children or commit
them to apprenticeships. Venture might also have been remembering the time
his mother left him to work for a rich farmer for a year. He also bought several
enslaved men. The first one ran away. Venture is unclear about the details.
He may have let the other two go free. In the end, these decisions were very
costly, especially when tragedy struck.

My wife and children were yet in bondage to Mr. Thomas Stanton.
About this time a chest containing, besides clothing, about 38 pounds in
paper money, was burned by accident in a fire. **A short time after I sold all**
my possessions in Stonington, consisting of a pretty piece of land and
one dwelling house. I went to find work on Long Island.

For the first four years, I spent my time in working for various people there and on **neighboring islands. In the space of six months I cut and corded upwards of 400 cords of wood.** In four years **I cut several thousand cords of wood, and the money which I earned thereby amounted to 207 pounds 10 shillings. This money I** carefully saved.

Perhaps some may enquire what I lived on all the time I was saving my money. I would inform them that I bought nothing which I did not absolutely want. All fine clothes I despised in comparison with my interest, and never kept but just what clothes were comfortable for common days, and perhaps I would have a garment or two which I did not have on at all times, but as for finery I never thought it to be compared with a decent homespun dress, a good supply of money, and <u>prudence</u>. Expensive gatherings of my mates I commonly shunned, and all kinds of luxuries I was perfectly a stranger to. During the time I was employed in cutting wood, I never was at the expense of six pence worth of spirits.

Being after this labor forty years of age, I worked at various places, and in particular on Ram Island, where I purchased Solomon and Cuff, two sons of mine, for 200 dollars each. I had saved considerable money, **amounting in all to near 300 pounds. When I had purchased my two sons, I had then left more than 100 pounds.**

After this I purchased an enslaved man, for no other reason than to oblige him, and gave for him 60 pounds. **But in a short time after he run away from me, and I thereby lost all that I** paid **for him,** except twenty pounds which he paid me previous to his running away.

The rest of my money I laid out in land, in addition to a farm which I owned before, with a **dwelling house** on it. Forty-four years had then com-

1767

1769

48

pleted their revolution since my entrance into this <u>existence of servitude and misfortune.</u>

Solomon, my eldest son, was seventeen years old and could work and earn money. I hired him out to Charles Church, of Rhode Island, for one year in exchange for twelve pounds and an opportunity of acquiring some learning.

1773

In the course of the year, Church fitted out a vessel for a whaling voyage, and, needing sailors, he enticed my son to go with the promise of giving him upon his return a pair of silver buckles besides his wages. As soon as I heard of his going to sea, I immediately set out to go and prevent it if possible. But on my arrival at Church's, to my great grief, I could only see the vessel my son was in almost out of sight going to sea.

My son died of the scurvy on this voyage, and Church has never paid me the least of his wages. In my son, besides the loss of his life, I lost equal to 75 pounds.

What is Scurvy?

Scurvy is a disease that sailors commonly died from. It is caused by a lack of Vitamin C in your diet. Vitamin C is found in citrus fruits and some vegetables.

Ships had to carry enough food on long voyages to feed the crew. Without refrigeration, ships carried little fresh food, and sailors had very poor diets. The connection between scurvy and eating a healthful diet that included fruits and vegetables was not understood until late in the 18th century.

CHAPTER 11:
VENTURE PURCHASES MEG'S FREEDOM

Today we marvel at the many ways that Venture made money. He was a businessman. He was his own boss. He was a trader, a farmer, and a fisherman. This is one way he was typical of many small landowners in colonial Connecticut.

Venture purchased Meg in 1773 or 1774. Surprisingly, though his son died on a whaling voyage, Venture signed on as a sailor on a whaling voyage organized by Oliver Smith. Working as a sailor was one of the few places white, black, and Native American men worked side by side. It was risky, though, for black sailors in particular. Sometimes they were sold into slavery in a port far from home. Venture was away for seven months. Meg took care of their farm and baby. Venture and Meg's last child, also named Solomon, was born in 1774. He was their only child who was born free.

While Venture and his family were living on Long Island, the town decided it did not want free black people to live there. The town passed an ordinance <u>expelling</u> *them from the town. Venture says that because he was a landowner, he and his family did not have to leave. Historians have not been able to figure out which town they lived in.*

My other son, being but a youth (Cuff was fifteen), still lived with me. About this time I chartered a <u>sloop</u>, and hired men to assist me in navigating her. I employed her mostly in the wood trade to Rhode Island, and

made clear of all my expenses above 100 dollars with her in better than one year.

Being in my forty-fourth year, I purchased my wife Meg, and thereby prevented having another child to buy, as she was then pregnant. I paid forty pounds for her.

During my residence at Long Island, I raised one year with another person ten cart loads of watermelons. I lost a great many every year by the thievishness of the sailors. What I made by selling watermelons amounted to nearly 500 dollars.

I worked at various things in order to enable me to purchase the rest of my family (Hannah). In the night time I fished with setnets and pots for eels and lobsters, and shortly after went on a whaling voyage in the service of Col. Smith. After being at sea seven months, the vessel returned laden with 400 barrels of whale oil.

About this time I bought another dwelling-house, and my affairs were in a pretty prosperous condition. This and my hard work was what alone saved me from being <u>expelled</u> on that part of the island in which I resided, as an act was passed by the select-men of the place, that all free black men should be expelled.

Next, after my wife, I purchased an enslaved man for 400 dollars. But he having an inclination to return to his old master, I therefore let him go. Shortly after I purchased another enslaved man for twenty-five pounds, whom I parted with shortly after.

Being about forty-six years old, I bought my oldest child Hannah, of Ray Mumford, for forty-four pounds, and she still resided with him. I had already redeemed from slavery myself, my wife and three children, besides three enslaved men.

® Michael Borders

52

CHAPTER 12: 100 ACRES IN CONNECTICUT

In 1774 Venture sold his land in Stonington and on Long Island and he, Meg, Cuff (age sixteen), and the younger Solomon (age one), moved to East Haddam, Connecticut. Venture does not say why he moved. One reason might have been that he needed to find forested land. Much of New England had been cleared of trees to allow for farming and to provide wood. Trees take a long time to re-grow.

It was also the eve of the Revolutionary War. Venture never mentions the war, but records show that his son Cuff served as a soldier in the 2nd Connecticut Regiment. Cuff, then in his early twenties, served from 1780 to 1783 and then returned home, married, and had a family of his own.

Venture began using the last name Smith. Records of his land purchases in Haddam list him as Venture Smith.

About the forty-seventh year of my life, I sold **all of my property on Long Island, and** moved to East Haddam. **I hired myself out at first to Timothy Chapman for five weeks, the earnings of which** I carefully saved. **After this I** worked **for Abel Bingham for about six weeks. I then put my money together and purchased** from **Bingham ten acres of land lying at Haddam Neck, where I now reside.**

On this land I labored with great diligence for two years, and shortly after purchased six acres more of land <u>contiguous</u> to my other. One year

_I775_

53

from that time (1777) I purchased 70 acres more of the same man, and paid for it mostly with the produce of my other land. Soon after I bought this last lot of land, I built a comfortable dwelling house on my farm with logs from my land.

Shortly after I had much trouble and expense with my daughter Hannah. She was married soon after I bought her to one Isaac, a free man, and shortly after her marriage she fell sick of a <u>mortal</u> disease. Her husband, a wretch, paid but little attention to her in her illness. I therefore thought it best to bring her to my house and nurse her there. I got her all the aid a man could afford. But in spite of this she died after much pain. The physician's bills amounted to forty pounds.

Having reached my fifty-fourth year, I hired two black men, one named William Jacklin, and the other Mingo. Mingo lived with me one year, and having received his wages, was in debt to me 8 dollars, for which he gave me his note. Presently he tried to run away from me without troubling himself to pay up his note.

I got a warrant, and requested he go to Justice Throop's on his own, but he refused. I took him on my shoulders, and carried him there, about two miles. The justice asked me if I had my prisoner's note with me, and replying that I had not, he told me that I must return with him and get it.

I carried Mingo back on my shoulders, but before we arrived at my dwelling, he complained of being hurt, and asked me if this was not a hard way of treating our fellow creatures.

I answered him that it would be hard thus to treat our honest fellow creatures.

He then told me that if I would let him off my shoulders, he had a pair of silver shoe buckles, one shirt, and a pocket handkerchief which he would turn out to me.

1781 *OR* 1782

I agreed, and let him return home with me on foot. But the following night, he slipped from me, stole my horse, and never paid me even his note.

The other man, Jacklin, being a comb-maker by trade, requested me to set him up in business and promised to reward me well with his labor. I bought him a set of tools for making combs, and supplies. He worked at my house about one year, and then run away from me with all his combs, and owed me for all his <u>board</u>.

Venture Smith's land on Haddam Neck as seen on a 1979 topological map.
State of Connecticut Highway Department, Library of Congress

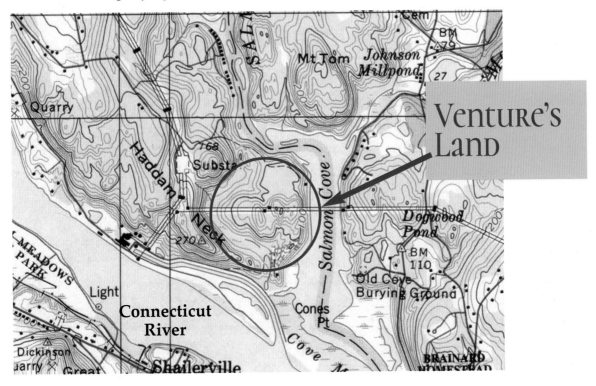

CHAPTER 13: CALLING OUT CHEATS AND COUNTING BLESSINGS

Since my residence at Haddam Neck, I have owned not less than twenty boats, including **canoes and sail vessels**. These I mostly employed in the fishing and trading business, and in these occupations I have been cheated out of considerable money by people whom I traded with taking advantage of my ignorance of numbers.

1786

About twelve years ago, I hired a whale-boat and four black men, and proceeded to Long Island after a load of round clams. Having arrived there, I first purchased of James Webb, son of Orange Webb, 660 clams, and afterwards, with the help of my men, finished loading my boat. The same evening, however, this Webb stole my boat, and went in her to the Connecticut River and sold her cargo for his own benefit. I pursued him, and at length, after an additional expense of nine crowns, recovered the boat. But for the proceeds of her cargo I never could obtain any <u>compensation</u>.

1790

Four years after, I met with another loss, far superior to this in value, and I think by no less wicked means. Being going to New London with a grandchild I took passage in an Indian's boat, and went there with him. On our return, the Indian took on board two <u>hogsheads</u> of molasses, one of which belonged to Capt. Elisha Hart of Saybrook, to be delivered on his wharf.

When we arrived there, and while I was gone at the request of the Indian to inform Captain Hart of his arrival and receive the freight for him, one hogshead of the molasses had been lost overboard in attempting to get it onto the wharf. Although I was absent at the time, as was known to a number of respectable witnesses, I was nevertheless prosecuted by Captain Hart (the Indian not being able to pay for it) and made to pay upwards of ten pounds lawful money with all the costs of the court. I asked the advice of several gentlemen, and they advised me, as Capt. Hart was rich and threatened to carry the matter from court to court till it would cost me more than the first damages, to pay the sum and accept responsibility. This I did, and he has often since insultingly taunted me with my unmerited misfortune. Such a proceeding as this, committed on a defenseless stranger, almost worn out in the hard service of the world, without any foundation in reason or justice, whatever it may be called in a Christian land, would in my native country have been branded as a crime equal to highway robbery. But Captain Hart was a white gentleman, and I a poor African, therefore it was all right, and good enough for the black dog.

1798

I am now sixty-nine years old. Though once straight and tall, measuring without shoes six feet one inch and a half, and every way well proportioned, I am now bowed down with age and hardship. My strength which was once equal if not superior to any man whom I have ever seen, is now enfeebled so that life is a burden, and it is with fatigue that I can walk a couple of miles, stooping over my walking stick. My eyesight has gradually failed, till I am almost blind, and whenever I go abroad one of my grandchildren must direct my way. For many years I have been much pained and troubled with an ulcer on one of my legs.

But amidst all my griefs and pains, I have many <u>consolations</u>. Meg, the wife of my youth, whom I married for love, and bought with my money is still alive. My freedom is a privilege which nothing else can equal.

Despite all of the losses I have suffered by fire, by the injustice of knaves, by the cruelty and oppression of false-hearted friends, and the <u>deceitfulness</u> of my own countrymen whom I have assisted and redeemed from bondage, I am now possessed of more than 100 acres of land, and three habitable dwelling houses. It gives me joy to think that I have and that I deserve so good a character, especially for truth and integrity.

While I am now looking to the grave as my home, my joy for this world would be full—IF my children, Cuff for whom I paid 200 dollars when a boy, and Solomon who was born soon after I purchased his mother—If Cuff and Solomon—O! that they had walked in the way of their father. But a father's lips are closed in silence and in grief!—<u>Vanity</u> of vanities, all is vanity!

The End.

CHAPTER 14:
HISTORIANS FILL IN THE BLANKS

Venture told his story to someone (we don't know who), and it was published by *The Bee* newspaper of New London. Venture tells us many details of his life, but he leaves many details out. Perhaps he told the things that were important to him, or the person writing down his story or the publisher only recorded what interested them about Venture's life.

Luckily, historians have researched many clues Venture left behind. They have been able to fill in some of the missing information that tells us about life in colonial Connecticut.

One example of the sources historians have used is records of the land that Venture bought and sold in Haddam from 1775 until his death in 1805. Haddam Town Hall contains records of land purchases and sales all the way back to Venture's time. These records are called land deeds.

Historian Cameron Blevins found twenty-nine land deeds in Haddam's town records with Venture's name on them. Blevins used Geographic Information System (GIS) software to map the land. This helped him discover what kind of land Venture owned. Some of it was flat and good for growing crops. Some was hilly and better for either chopping down trees or letting animals graze. He was able to visit Venture's land in person, too.

Venture first bought ten acres in Haddam Neck on the Salmon River in 1775. He bought a long, thin, hilly strip that dropped steeply down to the river's edge. The Salmon River was good for transportation and fishing. It was a tributary of the Connecticut River. This meant that Venture could easily travel by boat to Hartford, Middletown, and other river towns, and to cities and towns along Long Island Sound. With the land, he bought the right to stack wood on his neighbor's land and use his cart path to get to a flat area by the river to load wood to take to market.

Two years later Venture bought another seventy acres from the neighbor. He now owned the property with the cart path and the flat loading area on the river's edge. With the land he bought valuable fishing rights on the river. Venture did not have all of the money to make this purchase. He borrowed £55 from Timothy Chapman.

Venture built a house with logs he cut from the land. In 1778 Venture bought another 48 acres to the south of his property. By March 1778 he owned 134 acres. This is remarkable! Connecticut's average farmer owned between 80 and 120 acres of land. Venture had bought this land as a relative newcomer to the area, and after having to buy his freedom and his family's freedom.

Venture likely raised rye, wheat, and corn. He also planted apple trees. He had livestock, including cows, sheep, and pigs.

Venture now had more land than he and Cuff could work. Solomon was too young to be much help. In July 1778 Venture sold twelve acres of land to two free black men named Whacket and Peter for £66. It was a long strip similar to Venture's first piece of land.

Whacket had gained his freedom when his master died the year before. Earlier that spring he and Peter married free black women, Base and Peg, in a double wedding ceremony at East Haddam's Congregational church. Venture and Meg now had two young couples as neighbors and fellow workers. Town records from this period count only thirteen black people living in Haddam out of a population of 1,750, and 65 in neighboring East Haddam out of a population of 2,826.

Whacket and Peter did not stay long. Whacket sold his land to an East Haddam man named Amos White in 1780. Peter sold his land back to

Venture in 1781. The Revolutionary War was underway, and the economy was shaky. Venture stayed put and weathered the war in Haddam, while Whacket and Peter and their wives moved on.

After the war, in 1785, Venture finally paid off his mortgage to Timothy Chapman. He now owned his land free and clear. He also bought back the land Whacket had sold to White.

Venture and Meg's son Cuff returned from the war and settled on his family's land. He married and started a family. He worked much like his father and other men of the era. In addition to working for his father, he hauled stone from a nearby quarry and loaded boats.

In 1787 Venture, about sixty years old, started a new venture: he and William Ackley of East Haddam partnered in a fishing business. They built a place to fish using a seine in the Salmon River. A seine is a long net with floats at the top and sinkers weighing down the bottom. It hangs vertically in the water to catch fish.

Venture continued to borrow money when he needed it, and he paid it back on time. Those transactions show that many prominent white businessmen and farmers in Haddam and East Haddam were willing to do business with him. They trusted him to keep his end of the deal, and Venture trusted them to keep theirs.

Archaeologists have studied his property. They found evidence that Venture and Meg had a good-sized house for themselves. There were two other houses where Cuff and Solomon and their families lived. There were also warehouses, a blacksmith shop and forge, a dock, and a place to repair boats.

But Venture was getting older. Beginning in 1793 he began to sell land he could no longer work. In 1798 Venture sold three and a half acres to his son Solomon. This would give Solomon some security. There are no records showing that he did the same for his son Cuff.

Solomon eventually became the owner of the farm. Venture died in 1805 at age seventy-seven. His wife Marget (Meg) died in 1809 at age seventy-nine. Venture and Meg are buried in the cemetery at East Haddam's Congregational church. A large and decorative headstone marks Venture's grave. It says:

Sacred to the Memory of Venture Smith an African. Tho the son of a King he was kidnapped & sold as a slave but by his industry he acquired Money to purchase his Freedom who Died Sep 19th 1805 in the 77th year of his Age

Venture and Meg's headstones, First Church Cemetery,
East Haddam, 2018.

Photo: Elizabeth J. Normen

See photos of what archaeologists found at Venture Smith's homestead:

- diggingintothepast.org/venture-smith/
- venturesmithcolonialct.org/library

PART III

COLONIAL
CONNECTICUT

CHAPTER 15: CONNECTICUT'S BEGINNINGS

Across the region, more than a dozen Native American tribal groups had lived for more than 10,000 years. They spoke variations of the Eastern Algonquian language. The Mahikan, Weantinock, Pootatuck, Pequot, Mohegan, Quinnipiac, Wampanoag, Poquonnoc, Nehantic, Hammonasset, Wangunk, Tunxis, Paugusset, Pequannock, Wepawaug, and Siwanog lived in the area that became Connecticut.

In the early 1600s, the Dutch and other European traders made contact with Native people in the area we now call Connecticut. Early mapmakers recorded the areas where the different tribes lived.

Each tribe moved seasonally within its homelands to areas where food was plentiful. This migration is called the seasonal round. In the fall and winter tribes lived in more sheltered, wooded areas. This was the time for hunting. Groups of men hunted white-tailed deer. Deer meat was an important part of the Native diet. Deer skin and bone were used to make clothing and tools. Native Americans also hunted and ate birds and other animals. Fall and early winter were the time to gather nuts, roots, and tubers.

In the spring and summer, tribes moved to more open areas along rivers and the shoreline. Spring and summer were the seasons for planting corn, squash, and beans. Summer was a time to gather shellfish along Long Island Sound or to fish in rivers and ponds. Berries and edible plants were plentiful in summer. Native Americans were knowledgeable about the plants and animals around them.

previous page: Dress fabric (detail), c. 1732, hand-stiched embroidery in wool on linen. Connecticut Historical Society

Map showing location of Native American tribal groups around 1630. From John W. de Forest, *History of the Indians of Connecticut from the Earliest Known Period to 1850*, 1851.

In 1992 a 1,245-acre portion of the Mohegan Reservation, including more than 70 archaeological sites spanning 9,000 years of indigenous history, was designated a National Historical Landmark.
Source: Lucianne Lavin, *Connecticut's Indigenous Peoples*, 2013

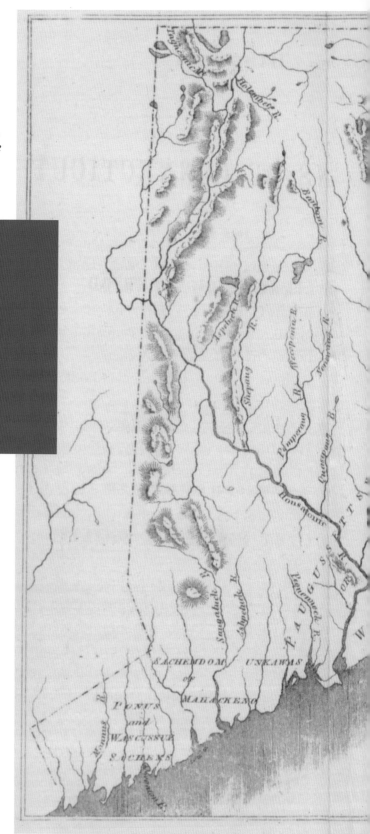

Connecticut.

IN

1630.

At their summer camps, Native Americans built round and oval wigwams. At their winter camps, they built larger, longer houses. A single family lived in a wigwam. More families could live together in the larger winter house. The structures were covered with tree bark or mats woven from rushes or cattails. The house of the sachem, the tribe's leader, was larger. It was used for meetings of tribal members and visitors from other tribes. Tribes traded with each other. They traded hides, clay pots, tobacco, maize, venison, and many other things.

Beliefs and cultures varied from tribe to tribe, but Native Americans in this region believed—and still do—in living in harmony with all living things. They believed everything has a spirit. Ceremonies, observed with song and dance, showed their respect for the animals, rocks, trees, and the cycle of the seasons. Sacred stories, told again and again, generation to generation, explained the beginning of the world and the connections between all living things. Children learned their culture through stories about Grandmother Woodchuck, Father Bear, Mother Earth, and the Three Sisters. Native Americans were astronomers, too. They looked to the sky and named constellations of stars.

The tribes in this region chose a leader, called a sachem, by consensus. The tribe would gather and agree as to who would be their leader. The sachem was often a man, and often a sachem's son would be chosen as the next sachem. Women could be sachem. A woman named Anne was named sachem (or sunksquaw) by the Mohegan in 1736. Mary Momoho was a sunksquaw of the Eastern Pequot.

Europeans Arrive

The Dutch were the first Europeans to explore the Connecticut River, beginning in 1614. They began trading with the Native Americans. They traded European-made goods for beaver pelts. Beaver pelts were prized in Europe, where they were used to make men's hats.

Wigwam at the Tantaquidgeon Museum in Uncasville.
Photo: Elizabeth J. Normen

Early European explorers found Indian settlements that were <u>fortified</u>. Dutch trader Adriaen Block reported that the Sequin had a fort near present-day South Windsor. A fort is a sign of a need for protection. The tribes may have fought each other over territory or <u>dominance</u>. Once the European traders arrived, the tribes fought over who would control trade with the Europeans. They also wished to show their strength to the Europeans. Their forts may have also been trading sites. Native Americans traded furs for European-made metal tools and utensils, guns, woven cloth, and glass and metal beads.

The Pequot established control over other tribes to the north and west. These other tribes had to pay <u>tribute</u> to the Pequot. Tribute might be paid in <u>wampum</u> or goods such as furs. The Pequot controlled the Native American fur trade.

Tribes to the west of the Connecticut River also were threatened by the powerful Mohawk. Threats from the Mohawk and Pequot led some tribes to welcome English settlement. They hoped the English would help protect them. In 1631 the Wangunk sachem Wahginnacut went to the Massachusetts Bay Colony to invite the English to settle in his territory.

The English began arriving in 1633. The first were Puritan ministers leading groups of families looking for a place to live where they could practice their religion in their own way.

The first English towns were established along the coast of Long Island Sound and major rivers. Hartford, Windsor, and Wethersfield were the first three towns. All three are on the Connecticut River. Waterways were important resources. They provided the easiest way to get from place to place. Rivers and streams offered fresh water to drink, fish and shellfish to eat, and water for crops.

The English learned from the Native Americans things that they needed to do to survive in the new world. But they had come to this new place to do things their way, and it wasn't long before there was conflict. Neither the English nor the Native Americans understood each other's customs and ways. They worshipped differently. They ate different foods. They dressed differently.

The English settlers didn't see or respect that the land they wished to settle was occupied. They saw only wilderness and opportunity for themselves. In some instances, the English believed they bought land from the local tribe. The Native Americans may have thought they were accepting gifts for sharing the land. Sometimes the English took the land without agreement with the local tribe. In every case, they made the tribe move away from the English settlements.

The two cultures had very different ideas about land ownership and how land should be used. Native American life depended on large land areas that tribes could access according to the season. Schaghticoke elder Trudie Richmond said, "We are taught that the land does not belong to the people, but rather the people belong to the land."

The English divided the land into lots for each family around a central common or green. They brought horses, cows, oxen, and pigs from England. These animals needed to be held in pens and pastures. The English built fences around their land. They built houses and barns. The English called this "improving" the land. They also dammed rivers and streams to power mills. These dams destroyed Native American fishing grounds.

The Native Americans resisted the disruption caused by the English settlers. Conflict and warfare between the tribes continued, too. The English were anxious to get control over the Native Americans. They wanted peace so that their settlements could grow and be successful.

The European brought three things that were particularly deadly to Native Americans: guns, disease, and alcoholic beverages. Native Americans had never been exposed to European diseases such as smallpox and cholera. Epidemics swept through Native communities in the 1630s. Historians estimate that disease killed 75 percent to 90 percent of the Native American population by 1656. Disease and the introduction of alcohol severely weakened Native communities.

Replica of Rev. Thomas Hooker's church. The original church was built in 1635. The replica shown here was built in 1935 to celebrate the state's 300th anniversary. At the lower left is a replica of stocks. People who committed crimes might be punished by being put in the stocks.
State Archives, Connecticut State Library

CHAPTER 16: BUILDING A PURITAN COLONY

In every town they founded, the Puritan settlers built a <u>meetinghouse</u> on the green. The church was the center of a Puritan town. Everyone in the town was required to attend church. People had to pay taxes to support the church and the minister. The meetinghouse was plain. Puritans didn't believe in fancy things. They didn't celebrate Christmas or Easter. The meetinghouse held town meetings and religious services.

Because of the threat of attack from the Pequot, Hartford, Windsor, and Wethersfield came together to form the Connecticut Colony in 1636. The Puritans set up a government. They wanted an orderly way to run the colony. One minister said, "Were it not for government, the world would soon run into all manner of disorders and confusions."

Colonial Government

Connecticut is very proud of its long history of independence. Unlike other colonies, Connecticut did not have a governor appointed by the King of England. The Connecticut Colony created a government the way they wanted it. They did this by adopting the Fundamental Orders in 1639.

The Fundamental Orders created a General Court. (It was called the General Assembly after 1698.) The General Court and the church governed the colony. The Puritan leaders did not believe that people could be good on their own. Early Connecticut was a very strict place!

The Puritans further believed that strong *family* government was important, too.

They wanted to be sure that every family followed the laws and worshipped God. The head of each family was required to lead the household in daily prayer. Indentured workers, apprentices, and enslaved people had to join in daily prayer, too. Children were taught to read so that they could read the Bible.

In 1650 the General Court adopted its first code of laws. The code did not include any laws about slavery, perhaps because there were so few enslaved people in the colony then. But slavery was accepted. The 1650 laws allowed for "hostile" Indians to be captured and "either to serve (be enslaved), or be shipped out and exchanged" for enslaved Africans.

The General Court appointed town constables to keep the peace, enforce laws, and supervise elections. People who committed crimes had to pay a fine, were publicly shamed by having to stand in the stocks, or were punished by being whipped, branded, or having part of an ear cut off. They could be held in the town jail. The state's first prison, New-Gate Prison in Simsbury (now East Granby), opened late in the colonial period in 1773.

Life in a Colonial Town

Today people choose where they want to live. In colonial Connecticut, people had to get permission to live in a town. The town leaders didn't want to include people who could not take care of themselves. If they didn't want you, you were "warned off" and had to find somewhere else to live.

Today all adult citizens, male and female, may participate in elections. But in colonial Connecticut, only the most successful men were allowed to vote and elect the leaders of the colony and the town. Colonial leaders thought this was the only way to ensure an orderly community. Only the "very best" men, those who were successful, pious landowners, could hold office. In New Haven, settled in 1638, only church members could vote. It would take nearly 300 years before everyone, including women and men, rich and poor, and people of any race or religion (or no religion), could participate in elections for the state's leaders or to run for office.

Towns in the colonial period were governed by town meeting. Many towns still practice this form of government. Men eligible to vote gathered a few times a year to conduct town business. They elected selectmen to oversee the town. The selectmen elected a moderator (like a mayor), a treasurer, and town clerk. The selectmen appointed men to do what was needed.

The Pequot War made it clear that towns had to be able to defend themselves. All white men sixteen years or older were required to be part of the local militia.

The Pequot War

Tensions began mounting between the settlers and the Native Americans when ten English traders were killed by their Niantic-Pequot guides in 1634. The Connecticut Colony demanded that the culprits be turned over to them. The Pequot argued that the murders were justified.

Violence continued. Settlers were killed by Pequot. The English killed Pequot. For several months, the Pequot attacked anyone who tried to leave the fort at Old Saybrook. More than twenty English were killed.

In April 1637 the Pequot attacked Wethersfield, killing nine men and two women and capturing two girls. On May 1 the General Court declared war. The English gathered militia and Native allies. Uncas, sachem of the Mohegan, allied with the English. The Pequot were his enemy. He wanted to get out from under the Pequot's control.

The English and their allies attacked the Pequot village of Mystick. They were brutal and nearly wiped out the Pequot.

The war showed the <u>folly</u> of violence against the English. Uncas showed the Mohegan's strength through alliance and negotiation with the English. But he also fought to gain power over other tribes.

The Connecticut Colony declared peace in a document called the Hartford Treaty of 1638. The treaty was made between the colony and its Native allies: Miantonomo, the Sachem of the Narragansetts, and Uncas, the Sachem of the Mohegans.

The Connecticut Colony took the Pequot homelands. Any Pequot survivors, the treaty said, "shall no longer be called Pequots." Some were enslaved and sent to the Caribbean. Those captured by the Mohegan or Narragansetts were to become part of their tribes.

The Connecticut Colony declared victory over all Native Americans within its borders even though Uncas and the Mohegan were its allies. Uncas found that the colonial leaders did not respect him as a political equal.

Life in a Native American Village

Every culture changes and adapts over time. The Native American tribes maintained their traditional culture and adopted new technologies such as metal cookware, iron tools, and metal arrow points. They defended their land against colonists who tried to settle on it. They protested to the colonial leadership when settlers' livestock got loose and damaged their crops.

Deer, bear, wild turkey, and beaver became over-hunted by the settlers. The Native Americans had to begin wearing clothing made of cloth and find new sources of meat. Because currency and coins were scarce in the colony, wampum became a form of money. The manufacture of wampum became an important industry for coastal tribes that had access to shells used to make it.

The Beginning of the Reservation System

Pequot survivors came together just a few years after the Pequot War. The Connecticut Colony assigned the Mashantucket Pequot a 500-acre reservation in the Noank section of Groton in 1651. It was rocky, hilly land, but it was on Long Island Sound and near favored fishing grounds.

Some Pequot moved inland to gain access to better farmland. Pequot Sachem Robin Cassacinamon I urged the colony to allot the Pequot more useful land. In 1666 the colony created a 3,000-acre reservation at Mashantucket.

Through the early 1670s the colonial Connecticut government relied heavily on its Native allies. Uncas worked with the Connecticut Colony to further the interests of the Mohegan people. As Uncas grew old, he wanted a guarantee that Mohegan land would remain in Mohegan hands forever. He asked the Connecticut General Assembly to set the boundaries of that land before he died. In 1671 20,000 acres of land were set aside for the Mohegans. This land encompassed thirty-two square miles between New London and Norwich.

In 1680 the Connecticut Colony passed a reservation law. That law said that any land set aside for Native Americans would be theirs forever. In 1683 500 acres were set aside in North Stonington for the Eastern or Paucatuck Pequot led by the sachem Wequash. The colony appointed British men to manage or oversee the reservations. But these men often worked for their own advantage and did not always protect the tribe they oversaw.

The Charter of 1662

Meanwhile colonial leaders had to watch what was happening in England. They got nervous about the colony's independence when a new king came to the English throne in 1660. The colony sent John Winthrop, Jr. to England in 1662. He asked the king for a royal charter. The resulting Charter of 1662 and the Fundamental Orders guided the colony's government until 1818. The charter merged Connecticut and New Haven into a single Connecticut Colony led by now-Governor Winthrop in 1665.

Governor John Winthrop, Jr.
Gov. Winthrop and his heirs owned Fishers Island, where Venture Smith spent his childhood enslaved.
State Archives, Connecticut State Library

King Philip's War

There was one final attempt by the Native Americans to drive the English out of New England. Metacomet, sachem of the Wampanoag (also known as King Philip), tried to unify Native American tribes across New England to wage war against the English. Some joined Metacomet, but Uncas remained allied with the Connecticut Colony and helped protect it from attack. Most of the fighting happened outside Connecticut, but Simsbury was burned to the ground. When Metacomet was killed in 1676, the war was over. Connecticut Native American tribes turned to diplomacy and appeals to the colonial General Assembly to fight for their rights.

A New King Threatens Connecticut

In 1686 England's new king, James II, put Connecticut and the other New England colonies, along with New York and New Jersey, under the rule of royal governor Sir Edmond Andros. He named the area the Dominion of New England. Luckily, just two years later a revolution in England brought a new king and queen into power. Andros was out, and Connecticut put its own government back in charge of the colony in 1689.

CHAPTER 17: GROWING PAINS

After King Philip's War, the British population grew rapidly. The colony was running out of land for the new settlers. The colonial government took it from the Native American reservations. Colonial leaders did not think the Indians needed as much land as they had because they did not "improve" it.

By 1705 New London, Colchester, and Lyme had claimed Mohegan land as part of their towns. In 1704 the Mohegans brought a lawsuit against the colony to make the colony honor the 1680 reservation law. They decided to appeal to a higher power. They sent their sachem Owaneco (Uncas's son) to England to petition Queen Anne. Queen Anne sided with the Mohegan. But the Connecticut Colony simply ignored her decision. The Mohegan lands were reduced to 5,000 acres in 1725.

British colonists wanted reservation land in Noank, too, and the colony took it away from the Mashantucket Pequot in 1714. This left the Pequot with their reservation at Mashantucket but cut them off from their important fishing grounds.

This pattern continued across the state. The Schaghticoke Reservation in Kent was established before 1736. It was about 2,000 acres. It was reduced to 400 acres in the 19th century and to just a quarter acre today. The Tunxis in the Farmington area fought the sale of their land by Sequassen, the sachem of the nearby Wangunk village of Sicoag. The Tunxis said the sale was illegal. They petitioned the General Assembly for 127 years, until 1767. Having lost their legal fight, in 1780 most of the tribe moved to western New York.

The many English settlers who arrived beginning in the early 1700s were not Puritans. The Puritans lost their strict control of towns. More towns were settled for economic reasons instead of religious ones. Rules began to relax. People still had to pay taxes to support the town's minister and what was now called the Congregational Church.

The colony continued to experience little royal interference. The final break with England came in 1776 when the American colonies fought the American Revolution.

Native Americans fought in colonial wars, including the American Revolution. Though nearly overcome by British settlement, Connecticut's first peoples survived and adapted while staying true to their ancestral homelands, culture, and traditional ways, which they continue to do today. Read about African American soldiers in the American Revolution in chapter 21.

Connecticut became a state in 1788.

Why is there a tree on Connecticut's quarter?

The story of the Charter Oak may be Connecticut's greatest legend. A legend is a story that many believe happened, but for which there is no proof.

For twenty years Connecticut operated under the Charter of 1662. (That much is true.) But, in 1685, King Charles II died. His brother, James II, became king. King James wanted more control over the colonies. He combined the New England colonies into one big colony called the Dominion of New England. He appointed Sir Edmund Andros governor.

Sir Andros demanded that all of the colonies turn in their charters. Connecticut's leaders refused to do so. Andros came to Hartford to seize Connecticut's charter.

On the evening of October 27, 1687, Andros met with the colony's leaders in Hartford at a local inn. The legend goes (this is the part that can't be proven!) that the charter lay on the table. All of a sudden, the candles blew out. The room was plunged into darkness. When the candles were lit again, the charter was gone!

Legend has it that Joseph Wadsworth took the charter from the table and ran. He hid it in the hollow of a large white oak tree on the property of George Wyllys, where Andros wouldn't be able to find it.

It was largely a <u>symbolic</u> act. With or without the charter, Connecticut became part of the Dominion of New England. The General Court was disbanded. Two years later a revolution took place in England, and King William III and Queen Mary II came to power. They allowed the colonies to govern themselves. Connecticut recovered the charter from the oak and governed itself as it had before.

The legend of the Charter Oak began to be told 100 years later, just after the Revolutionary War. Because it showed Connecticut's fierce independence, the story was wildly popular.

Source: "Exploiting the Legend of the Charter Oak" by David Corrigan, *Connecticut Explored*, Winter 2007-2008.

CHAPTER 18: THE COLONIAL ECONOMY

The first English settlers had to build towns from the ground up. They felled the trees to clear the land for pastures and fields and built houses and barns. They could buy goods from England, but those goods were expensive. Colonists made and grew most of what they needed. They traded what they didn't need with the Native Americans and other settlers.

The colonists set up small industries such as gristmills and sawmills. Mills could be built along Connecticut's small rivers and fast-moving streams. The power of the rushing water moved the millstones to grind grain into flour. Waterpower moved saw blades to cut logs into lumber.

There was so much to do to build new towns. There were not enough workers, and the cost in wages to hire workers went up. Slavery took hold. (See Part IV.) Parents often apprenticed their children to learn a trade or indentured their children to work. Even Venture Smith would do this, too, with his oldest son.

Money was scarce in the young colony, so people bartered, trading their goods or labor for something they needed in return. Settlers could pay their taxes in corn and other products. (See page 32.) Wampum became a form of money.

The typical settler raised corn, wheat and other grains, horses, cattle, pigs, and sheep. Cattle could be used to plow a field, or for transportation, food, and hides. A garden near the settler's house provided vegetables, and orchards provided fruit. Apple trees were imported from England.

The cycle of the seasons ruled the day: planting in the spring, tending crops in the summer, and harvesting in the fall. Animals had to be fed and cared for daily. Animals bred for meat were slaughtered in the fall or taken to market to be sold.

Year-round, fires for cooking needed firewood, and water had to be carried from the well to the house several times a day. Laundry was a back-breaking task. If someone needed a new shirt or skirt, first the cloth had to be made. Then the garment was sewn by hand. Colonists were shoemakers, candle makers, and toolmakers. Their work was never done.

What people couldn't make they could buy at the weekly market in Hartford. New Haven held a market, too, though at first it was held just twice a year.

Connecticut's forests provided wood for heat and cooking, lumber to build houses, boats, and barrels, and tar and pitch used in boat-building. Venture Smith found the sale of wood to be a good way to earn money.

The fur trade and fishing offered ways to make money. In the early years of the colony, most of the trading took place locally and in the region. Later, trade would expand to the Caribbean and the west coast of Africa. (See Part IV.)

Children's Role in the Colonial Economy

The Connecticut General Court required parents to teach their children how to read, and to teach them the Bible and the laws of the colony. Children were required to learn how to work. Parents put their children to work at a very young age, helping on the family's farm or in its business. Children were also sent to live with other families to learn a trade or a skill. Children went to school a few weeks or months a year and usually stopped going to school by age twelve. A small number of young men could go to Yale College in New Haven, which was founded in 1701.

CHAPTER 19:
SLAVERY IN COLONIAL CONNECTICUT

Pequots captured during the Pequot War were enslaved. The first enslaved African was captured and brought to the colony around 1639. At first, only a few English settlers purchased slaves. They mistakenly saw Africans and Native Americans as less than human. The introduction to Venture's story says that he had no reason "to suppose himself superior to the beasts, his fellow servants."

Connecticut had mostly small family farms. If a family owned slaves, it usually owned one or two enslaved people. These could be men, women, or children who were often separated from their families. Merchants, ministers, lawyers, and farmers owned enslaved people.

As time went on, more enslaved people were brought to Connecticut. There are examples of people who owned as many as twenty-five slaves, including Elijah Mason of Lebanon, Godfrey Malbone of Pomfret, and John Perkins of Norwich. Captain George Mumford, who became one of Venture's owners, had as many as twenty-five slaves when he died in 1755.

In the 1700s Connecticut prospered from coastal trading with other American colonies and in the West Indies. The West Indies used huge numbers of enslaved people to work the islands' sugar plantations. The landowners could make more money growing sugar cane than growing food. They imported crops, livestock, and lumber from Connecticut and other American colonies instead of producing those things themselves. Connecticut

Detail, "The First, Second, and Last Scene of Mortality," by
Prudence Punderson, 1776-1783, silk embroidery and ink on silk cloth.
Connecticut Historical Society

merchants loaded their ships with goods for market in the Caribbean and returned with sugar products they used to make rum.

Some Connecticut ship owners and ship captains sailed to Africa to purchase slaves. From there they sailed to the Caribbean to sell their human cargo and returned to Connecticut with a few enslaved Africans and sugar products to sell locally. This was called the "Triangle Trade."

Venture Smith was caught up in the Triangle Trade. The ship he was brought to America on may have been the *Little George* or the *Charming Susanna*. Captain James Collingwood and the *Little George* were in West Africa in 1736. Records show that two years later Collingwood sailed the *Charming Susanna* from Rhode Island to West Africa, where he traded its cargo for enslaved men, women, and children. The *Charming Susanna* then sailed to Barbados, where the captain sold the enslaved people before returning to Rhode Island with cargo it picked up in Barbados. Collingwood seems to have quit the slave trade after that and to have become a privateer. A privateer is like a pirate who works for the government. A privateer would try to capture an enemy ship and take its cargo for the colonial government.

(detail) Waterfront view of Bridgetown, Barbados, 1695. Library of Congress

Life in Colonial Connecticut for Enslaved Africans

During the colonial period enslaved Africans could be found scattered across the Connecticut Colony. They were separated from their families and isolated from other Africans. In their homeland, families were close-knit. Villages and tribes were made up of large extended families. In Africa everyone in a village shared a family history and belonged. Early in colonial Connecticut, though, it was rare for an African to meet another African. If he did, that person was likely from a different African village and a different ethnic group. Their native languages might be similar but not the same.

The English colonists expected enslaved Africans to give up their culture and religion. The Africans were expected to learn to do things as their owners wanted them done and to become Christian. But the African men and women did not forget the culture and religion of their homeland. They remembered their music and knowledge of instrument-making, for example. They could make and play fiddles, flutes, banjos, tambourines, and drums.

Enslaved Africans brought with them skills they learned in their homeland, such as farming, cattle herding, hunting, fishing, cooking, and basket-weaving. Some had knowledge and skills in herbal medicine and knew how to prevent smallpox and other diseases.

Enslaved Africans learned the skills and trades needed to survive in colonial Connecticut, too: farming, brick-making, barrel-making, mining, masonry, ship-building, and shoe-making, to name just a few occupations. They became skilled at many things, but they were not given a formal education. Few enslaved people were taught math or to read and write.

Life was very hard for enslaved men and women. They were given the hardest tasks to do. They suffered crippling injuries from their work. Venture tells us how his long days of hard work affected him as an old man.

Enslaved people generally had poor diets. Good nutrition in the colonial era was difficult for everyone, especially in the winter, when fresh vegetables and fruit were not available. Enslaved people and indentured workers only got to eat what was left over after their owners had eaten.

Enslaved people slept in attics and cellars that were cold in the winter and stifling hot in the summer. Venture tells of sleeping on the hearth in the winter with just a thin blanket under him and a thin cover over him.

Enslaved women in colonial Connecticut worked in and around the house. This was hard labor. They had to carry heavy jugs of water from the well to the kitchen several times a day. They had to move heavy pots from the cooking fire to the table. Laundry was particularly hard work. They had to fill heavy cauldrons with water and build a fire to heat the water. Soap was made from lye and animal fat. The clothes were boiled and then wrung out by hand and hung up to dry. Dry clothes were then ironed with heavy irons that had been heated in the fire.

Venture tells us very little about his wife Meg. We know she endured many years of slavery. She was often separated from her husband, and she cared for her children in addition to doing the work she was required to do for her master and mistress.

Black Governors

For at least 100 years, from about 1749 to 1856 or so, free and enslaved black people in Connecticut had a custom of electing a leader. The practice reached back to customs and traditions in Africa. The community came together and chose a leader. Sometimes the leader was chosen by voice vote. Sometimes the election was decided through a test of physical strength. Elections were sometimes celebrated with a parade. A man named Hercules may have been the first "Black Governor," as these leaders were known. He was elected by the African and African American community in New London in the 1740s.

The Black Governor was not a position recognized by the Connecticut General Assembly. Leaders seem to have been chosen for their good character and commitment to help their community.

Peter Freeman of Farmington was elected a Black Governor in 1780 when he was twenty-eight years old. He was a Black Governor for several years. He was a veteran of the Revolutionary War. Born to enslaved parents from Middletown, he had purchased his freedom. He and his father, Cuff Freeman, owned a large, 94-acre farm in Farmington, where they grew wheat and rye. He was described in *The Hartford Courant* (February 1851) a few years before his death as a good citizen who had served honorably in the Revolutionary War.

"The First, Second, and Last Scene of Mortality," by Prudence Punderson, 1776-1783, silk embroidery and ink on silk cloth. Connecticut Historical Society

CHAPTER 20: LAWS ABOUT SLAVERY

In 1678 it was estimated that there were about 30 enslaved people in the Connecticut Colony. By 1700 Connecticut's total population had grown to 30,000 people. It was estimated that about 1 in 10 families in Connecticut owned slaves. By the time Venture arrived in the American colonies in 1739, 1 in 4 families owned slaves. Connecticut's population of enslaved people was about 2,600 and growing fast.

As the number of enslaved people in the colony increased, the General Assembly passed laws to control and regulate slavery and enslaved people. Slaves could not travel beyond town borders (1690) and could not be outside after dark (1723). Fearful of runaways, the colony required ferry operators to check that a person of color had a pass that allowed him to take the ferry across the river.

Whites became fearful as the number of free blacks increased in the colony. They were afraid that free black people couldn't take care of themselves and would become a burden on the town. This fear ignored the fact that black people had been doing the hard work of farming and many other jobs and raising families for years, just like white people. In 1717 people in New London protested against a free black man named Robert Jacklin who lived in town and purchased land. They petitioned the General Assembly to make a law saying no free black person could buy land or live in a town without the town's permission. This law would make it very hard for a man like Jacklin to be successful. The law was not passed.

In 1761 a young man named Caesar Sambo was jailed for traveling without a pass in Litchfield. He said he was free, but an ad placed in the *Connecticut Gazette* advertised for his owner to claim him. If no owner appeared, the ad said he would be indentured to pay the costs of being jailed. Sambo found freedom hard to hold onto. His freedom could easily be taken away by a white person saying he was a runaway slave.

In New England enslaved people were allowed to sue and defend themselves in court (1730). This means they had some legal rights. New England courts usually (but not always) sided with the owner. Venture shows us an example. He appealed to the local justice when one of his masters beat him. The justice only warned his master not to mistreat Venture.

But some enslaved men and women did get justice. In a case similar to Caesar Sambo's in 1788, Jack Randall of Norwich was attacked by two white men who argued that he had been out of town without a pass. They said he was a runaway slave. Randall said he was a free man. He charged that the two men were trying to kidnap him to sell him into slavery. Randall won his case.

Others were able to win their freedom through the courts. They argued that they were enslaved illegally, and in some cases the court agreed.

The General Assembly was concerned about who would care for old, sick, or disabled slaves and former slaves. It passed a law in 1702 requiring owners to be responsible for anyone they had owned when they became elderly or disabled. This was good and bad. On the good side, an owner could not free an enslaved person just because he or she couldn't work anymore. That would leave people unable to support themselves. But the bad side was that it kept people enslaved longer, perhaps for their whole lives.

In 1774 Connecticut outlawed bringing enslaved people into the colony to sell them. The law to end the slave trade was passed for two reasons. One reason was that by the late 1700s there wasn't a need for enslaved labor. There were enough colonists to fill jobs. White men began to resent enslaved people for taking jobs. The economy was not strong.

There was no longer an economic reason for slavery in Connecticut.

The second reason was that in the era of the American Revolution, people were feeling the spirit of freedom and American independence. Public opinion began to turn against slavery. This ad in *The Hartford Courant* from 1783 shows, however, that sales of enslaved people continued. These two ads are for a thirty-five-year-old woman and her baby and a twelve-year-old girl.

TO BE SOLD,

A GOOD healthy Negro WENCH, about 35 years of age, who understands all kinds of house work, with a female Child 8 months old, enquire of the Printers.
Hartford, April 5, 1783.

TAKE NOTICE,

TO be sold a very likely spry active Negro GIRL, about twelve years old, enquire of the Subscriber.

JOHN KIRBY.

Middletown, March 15, 1783.

CHAPTER 21: SLAVERY AND THE AMERICAN REVOLUTION

The American Revolution helped many enslaved men and women gain their freedom. There were several paths to freedom. One was to join the British—the enemy against which the American patriots were fighting. The British offered to free any enslaved person who joined their side.

Second, some slave owners loyal to the British left Connecticut and went to loyalist areas. Sometimes they left their slaves behind. The enslaved people left behind could run away. They could turn to free black people for help. Evidence seems to show that more white people were willing to help them, too, instead of turning them in. Reverend Samuel Peters of Hebron is one example of a loyalist who left Connecticut during the war. He and his family fled to England, leaving his slaves Caesar and Lois behind. (Read more about their story on page 95.)

Third, some enslaved men got their freedom by fighting for the American patriots. The General Assembly passed a law allowing slave owners to send their enslaved men to serve in their place if they gave them their freedom. The law also freed the owner from having to take care of the former slave if he was injured or got sick.

Cuffee Wells fought in the American Revolution. He, like Venture, was born in Africa, enslaved, and brought to Connecticut as a child. In 1777 he enlisted in the Continental Army. He was a private in the 4th Connecticut Regiment. He knew about medicine. He probably learned from his first master, who was a doctor. During the war he assisted an army doctor in Danbury and at Valley Forge. After the war, his owner did not free him. Wells used his army pay to buy his freedom. He married and bought three acres of land in Lebanon.

The Battle of Groton

In 1781 the British, led by General Benedict Arnold, attacked New London. They set the town on fire to destroy patriot supplies stored there. The town's militia rallied to defend New London and Groton across the Thames River. One hundred and fifty militiamen gathered at Fort Griswold in Groton.

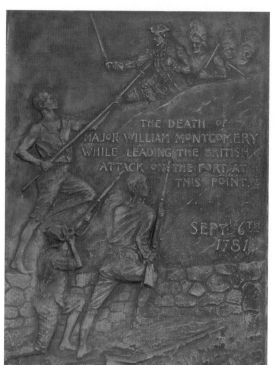

Among them were Latham Lambert and Jordan Freeman. Both were enslaved. Their owners were officers in the local militia.

The Americans were outnumbered. The British had more than 800 men. British Major Montgomery led the redcoats up and over the fort's embankments. The militia fought back. Freeman killed Montgomery with a spear. In the fighting, Freeman was also killed.

The British overtook the fort and killed most of the patriots. Lambert was among those killed. Freeman and Lambert served the patriot cause as enslaved men and died before they were freed. Their service is commemorated on a plaque at Fort Griswold.

After the Revolution, free black people moved to seaports to find work. The population of free blacks swelled in those port cities.

Plaque honoring the service of Latham Lambert and Jordan Freeman at the Battle of Groton during the Revolutionary War.
photo: Elizabeth J. Normen

Read more about Cuffee Wells at gilderlehrman.org/content/former-slave-doctor-cuffee-wells-1781.

Caesar and Lois Peters

Caesar was captured and brought to Connecticut as an eight- or nine-year-old boy around 1758. Lois's story is not known. By the American Revolution they were enslaved to Reverend Samuel Peters in Hebron. In 1774 Reverend Peters left Hebron because of his loyalty to England. He went to London, England, leaving Caesar and Lois behind.

The couple continued to live on and work Peters's farm. But the colony considered the farm abandoned and took it. The colony rented it out to another farmer. Caesar and Lois had to leave. They made a home for themselves nearby and continued to support themselves.

After the war Peters's farm was once again abandoned. Caesar and Lois moved back to the farm. They worked hard and paid the taxes on the property.

Suddenly, in September 1787, six armed men showed up. They came to take Caesar, Lois, and their family and sell them to pay Rev. Peters's debts. The family was thrown into the back of a wagon. Caesar was put in iron shackles.

Neighbors heard their cries and the commotion. They came running and asked what was going on. The men, weapons drawn, showed papers giving them the right to take the family away.

The people of Hebron were outraged at the cruelty and unfairness. They decided to try to rescue the family.

Just before the slave catchers and their captives reached Norwich and a ship bound for South Carolina, the rescuers succeeded in their quest. But Caesar and Lois's troubles were not over. Were they still the property of Rev. Peters? The case went to court. In January 1789 the General Assembly heard the petitions of the people of Hebron calling for the family to be freed. The General Assembly agreed, and Caesar, Lois, and their family were freed.

Source: "Caesar and Lois Peters" by Peter Hinks,
African American Connecticut Explored

CHAPTER 22:
THE END OF SLAVERY IN CONNECTICUT

The American Revolution helped convince Connecticut to end slavery. It was a long, drawn-out process that did not end until 1848. Prime and Prince, both enslaved men in Fairfield, petitioned the General Assembly in 1779. Their petition said "Although our skins are different in color from those we serve, ... we ... can never be convinced that we were made to be slaves." The General Assembly rejected petitions to end slavery in 1777, 1779, and 1780.

But the spirit of the American Revolution began to change people's minds. Connecticut passed a Gradual Emancipation Act in 1784. It did not free any slaves right away. It only freed babies born into slavery after they reached twenty-five years of age. Rhode Island also passed a gradual emancipation law in 1784. Connecticut, Rhode Island, and New Hampshire were the last of the New England states to end slavery.

According to the first federal census taken in 1790, there were no slaves in Massachusetts or Vermont, New Hampshire counted 157 enslaved people, Rhode Island counted 958, and Connecticut had the most: 2,648. (Maine was then part of Massachusetts; it didn't become a state until 1820.)

Connecticut repealed its earlier laws restricting African Americans' rights in 1797.

When Did Each New England State and New York End Slavery?

State	Date Slavery Ended	How It Was Ended
Vermont	1777	Slavery was outlawed in the state's constitution passed in 1777.
Massachusetts (including the area that became Maine)	No definite date	After Massachusetts adopted a state constitution in 1780 that said, "All men are born free and equal," several enslaved people won lawsuits saying that they were free under the state constitution. But slavery continued for a time anyway. The federal census of 1790 recorded no slaves in Massachusetts.
New Hampshire	No definite date	New Hampshire adopted a state constitution in 1783 that said, "All men are born free and equal," but a judge there said it did not apply to enslaved people or only those born after 1783. The 1790 census recorded 157 enslaved people in New Hampshire.
Rhode Island	1843	Rhode Island adopted a gradual emancipation law in 1784 and outlawed slavery in its state constitution, adopted in 1843. Article 1, section 4 of the constitution stated simply, "Slavery shall not be permitted in this state."
Connecticut	1848	A gradual emancipation law was passed in 1784. The state's constitution, adopted in 1818, did not use language like Massachusetts and New Hampshire did about natural rights and is silent about slavery. Slavery was outlawed in 1848.
New York	1827	A gradual emancipation law passed in 1799. A law passed in 1817 abolished slavery but not until 1827. The federal census reported 21,000 enslaved people in 1790 (6 percent of the population), and 10,000 in 1820 (less than 1 percent of the population).

Finding Freedom in Colonial Connecticut

African and African American men and women made a place for themselves in Connecticut from the earliest days of the colony. Philip and Ruth Moore are one early example. Little is known about this family except that when Philip died in Hartford in 1695 he was free. He owned several pieces of property, including a house in what is now East Hartford. He had a wife, grown children, and grandchildren. His wife Ruth inherited his property. She was an early example of a free black woman in the Connecticut Colony who owned property.

Enslaved men and women became free by buying their freedom (like Venture), by having their owners free them, by running away, or by suing the General Assembly to prove they were illegally enslaved. Newspaper ads show that many enslaved people ran away. Records also show that some masters freed their slaves in their wills. (A will gives instructions about what to do with your property and money after you die.)

Though the black population in colonial Connecticut was small (never more than 3 percent of the colony's total population), at the time of the American Revolution Connecticut had the largest number of enslaved people—more than 5,000—of any colony in New England (though that number was much smaller than in New York). The part of Connecticut with the largest number of enslaved people was New London County. New London was a thriving port city.

As time went on, though, the number of Africans and African Americans who were free increased. When Venture arrived in Connecticut, it is estimated that one in six were free. By the American Revolution, one in four blacks were free. By 1800, nearly nine out of ten African Americans were free.

In 1848, when slavery was finally ended by law in Connecticut, there may not have been any enslaved people in the state. It had been sixty-four years since the Gradual Emancipation Act had passed.

1790 Federal Census

	Enslaved Blacks	Percent of the Population	Free Blacks	Percent of the Population
New York	21,193	6.2	4,682	1.4
Connecticut	2,648	1.1	2,771	1.2
Rhode Island	958	1.4	3,418	5.0
New Hampshire	157	.1	630	.4
Massachusetts	0	0	5,639	1.4
Vermont	0	0	269	.3

* Maine was not a state until 1820. It was part of Massachusetts.

Connecticut : Free vs. Enslaved

🧍Free   🧍Enslaved

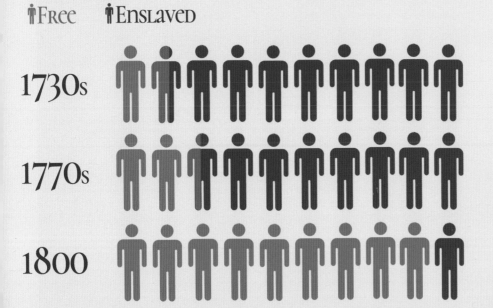

1730s

1770s

1800

Nancy Toney of Windsor may have been the last enslaved person in Connecticut. She was born in 1774 in Fairfield. She was ten years old when the Gradual Emancipation Act was passed, so it did not apply to her. When she was eleven she was given to Charlotte Bradley as a wedding present. She was separated from her family because her new mistress's new husband lived in Windsor. Nancy was likely freed sometime between 1821 and 1830 when she was in her fifties. She continued to live with the family that had enslaved her until her death at age eighty-two in 1857.

Portrait of Nancy Toney by Osbert Burr Loomis, c. 1862. Loomis Chaffee School Archives

CHAPTER 23:
WHY VENTURE'S STORY IS IMPORTANT

One important thing we must acknowledge about America's founding is that the white founders wanted independence and the right to pursue life, liberty, and happiness, but at the same time they denied those rights to Africans and Native Americans.

The experience of Native Americans and Africans is not the same. There is, however, a common thread of being denied equal access to the rights colonial settlers had. They were denied the same human dignity and human rights. That is a <u>legacy</u> we are still working to overcome today.

Once slavery ended, life did not get easier for African Americans. White people's attitudes hardened against black people. One example involves the right to vote and become full citizens. In the colonial era, the right to vote was restricted to men who were successful. As a landowner, Venture would have qualified to vote in colonial Connecticut. But he does not talk about voting or his role in the civic life of Haddam.

After the American Revolution, two formerly enslaved men in Wallingford, like Venture, owned enough property to qualify to vote. They did get the right to vote. Jack John was admitted as a freeman (a voter) in 1799, and Toby Birdseye in 1803.

The qualifications for voting were loosened around the time the state adopted its first state constitution in 1818. Before then, it was estimated that fewer than half of white men qualified to vote. The state lowered the property requirement, which meant that more men qualified to vote. But in 1814 the General Assembly passed a law restricting voting in Connecticut to white men. Just as more free blacks owned enough property to qualify to vote, a state law excluded them by race.

Black people did not accept this. Groups of black men and women sent petitions to the General Assembly twenty-six times between 1814 and 1850 arguing for voting rights. Each time their petition was rejected. Black men did not get the right to vote in Connecticut until 1876 after the passage of the Fifteenth Amendment to the United States Constitution in 1870. Women did not get the right to vote until the passage of the Nineteenth Amendment to the U.S. Constitution in 1920.

The 19th century was a time of great change in Connecticut. The state's agricultural and market economy was transformed by the industrial revolution. The primarily British-American population (with small African- and Native-American populations) added a large influx of Irish immigrants, followed by Italians, Germans, and Scandinavians. By the end of the 19th century, slavery was outlawed in Connecticut (1848) and, after a devastating civil war, in the rest of the United States (1865).

Though African Americans remained a small percentage of the population in Connecticut, in the early 1800s they began to form communities and found churches and schools. They rallied in support of the Amistad captives and formed societies to end slavery throughout the United States. They fought for their civil rights.

Prominent African American leaders emerged, including ministers James Pennington and Amos Beman, New Haven builder and entrepreneur William Lanson, photographer Augustus Washington, poet Ann Plato, teacher Rebecca Primus, artist Charles Ethan Porter, and ambassador Ebenezer Bassett, among many others. Though they continued to face hostility and racism, African Americans claimed their rightful place in the new State of Connecticut.

Learn more at Connecticutfreedomtrail.org.

Another Voice from the Past
Reverend Samson Occom

Samson Occom was a Mohegan. He lived around the same time as Venture Smith. He was born in 1723 and died in 1792. Like Venture, he wrote about his life. In a short piece he wrote in 1765, he described his childhood (his words are in bold and this is his spelling and punctuation):

My parents Liv'd a wandering life, as did all the Indians at Mohegan; they Chiefly Depended upon Hunting Fishing & Fowling for their Living and had no Connections with the English, excepting to trade **with them in their Small Trifles,—and they Strictly maintain'd and follow'd their ... Ways, Customs & Religion—tho' there was Some** English ministers preaching Christianity **among them. ... and when I was about 10 Years of age there was a man who went about among the Indian Wigwams, and where ever he Could find the Indian Childn, he would make them read— but the Children Usd to take Care to keep out of his way;—and he Us'd to Catch me Some times and make me Say over my Letters, and I believe I learnt Some of them. But this was Soon over too—and all this Time there was not one amongst us, that made a Profession of Christianity—Neither did we Cultivate our Land, nor kept any Sort of Creatures except Dogs, Which We Used in Hunting; and Dwelt in Wigwams, These are a Sort of Tents, Coverd with Matts—And to this Time we were unaquainted with the English Toung in General tho there were a few, who understood a little of it.**

As a young man, Occom was inspired to become a Christian minister. He became a missionary. A missionary lives among people of another culture and tries to get them to change to their religion. Occom worked his whole life to help the Mohegan and other Native peoples, but life as a missionary had many challenges. Read more about Occom at VentureSmithColonialCT.org/library.

GLOSSARY

Almighty protector
God

arrogantly
showing you feel you are better
than someone else

board
live and have meals in a house in
return for payment or service

commodities
goods, something that is
bought and sold

compensation
payment

consensus
agreement shared by all of the
people in the group

consolation
comfort after a loss

contiguous
adjoining, next to each other

currency
money that a country uses

custody
locked up, in jail

deceitfulness
dishonesty

dominance
control over

emancipation
being given one's freedom

ethnic
sharing a common culture
or set of traditions

**existence of servitude and
misfortune**
life of serving others and
experiencing great hardships

expel
force someone to leave

folly
foolishness, lack of good sense

fortified
protected against attack

hogshead
a large barrel

legacy
what one leaves behind,
especially after death

maize
corn

meetinghouse
building used as a church and
for town meetings

mortal
causing death

pious
religious

prudence
taking great care

rash
careless

reservation
area where the government forces
groups of Native Americans to live

sachem
the leader of a tribe

scholars
people who study and learn a
great deal about a topic

sloop
a type of sailboat

speculate
take business risks

symbolic
making a statement, representing
an idea

traumatic
something that is very harmful,
shocking, or upsetting

tribute
a forced payment

trifle
not very important

tuber
root vegetable

vanity
too much pride in oneself

wampum
beads made of quahog and whelk
shells

wigwam
round or oval home of sticks and
bark where Native Americans lived

SOURCES

Adams, Catherine and Elizabeth H. Pleck. *Love of Freedom: Black Women in Colonial and Revolutionary New England*. Oxford University Press, 2010.

Blevins, Cameron. "'Owned by Negro Venture': Land and Liberty in the Life of Venture Smith," in James Brewer Stewart, ed., *Venture Smith and the Business of Slavery and Freedom*. University of Massachusetts Press, 2010.

Bushman, Richard. *From Puritan to Yankee: Character and the Social Order in Connecticut, 1690 – 1765*. Harvard University Press, 1967.

Corrigan, David. "Exploiting the Legend of the Charter Oak," *Connecticut Explored*, Winter 2007 – 2008.

Daniels, Bruce. *The Connecticut Town: Growth and Development, 1635 – 1790*. Wesleyan University Press, 1979.

Den Ouden, Amy E. *Beyond Conquest: Native Peoples and the Struggle for History in New England*. University of Nebraska Press, 2005.

Farrow, Anne, Joel Lang, and Jenifer Frank. *Complicity: How the North Promoted, Prolonged, and Profited from Slavery*. Ballantine Books, 2005.

Finlay, Nancy. "The Importance of Being Puritan: Church and State in Colonial Connecticut," Connecticuthistory.org, https://connecticut history.org/the-importance-of-being-puritan-church-and-state-in-colonial-connecticut/.

Glaza, Tobias and Paul Grant-Costa. "Breaking the Myth of the Unmanaged Landscape," *Connecticut Explored*, Spring 2012.

Harris, Katherine J. "In Remembrance of Their Kings of Guinea: The Black Governors and the Negro Election, 1749 to 1780," *African American Connecticut Explored*. Wesleyan University Press, 2014.

Harris, Katherine J. "Black Governors, 1780 to 1856," *African American Connecticut Explored*. Wesleyan University Press, 2014.

Hinks, Peter. "Caesar and Lois Peters," *African American Connecticut Explored.* Wesleyan University Press, 2014 and https://connecticuthistory. org/changing-sentiments-on-slavery-in-colonial-hebron/.

Holsey, Bayo. *Routes of Remembrance: Refashioning the Slave Trade in Ghana.* The University of Chicago Press, 2008.

Lavin, Lucianne. *Connecticut's Indigenous Peoples: What Archaeology, History, and Oral Traditions Teach Us About Their Communities and Cultures.* Yale University Press, 2013.

Lavin, Lucianne. *Peter Freeman and Whacket Freeman: Towards an Archaeology of 18th Century Black Homesteads*. Institute of American Indian Studies, 2012, accessed at https://www.iaismuseum.org/wp-content/uploads/2017/02/venture-smith.pdf.

Lavin, Lucianne. "More Exciting Discoveries at the Venture Smith Archaeology Site," *Connecticut Preservation News*, January/February 2008. https://www.iaismuseum.org/wp-content/uploads/2017/02/cpn-jan-2008.pdf.

Lavin, Lucianne and Marc Banks. *The Venture Smith Homestead*. Connecticut Commission on Culture and Tourism and the Connecticut State Museum of Natural History/Connecticut Archaeology Center, 2010.

Leach, Eugene. "The Life and Adventures of Venture, a Native of Africa," *Connecticut Explored*, Winter 2012/2013.

Leach, Eugene. "Milford, Guilford, and Stratford at 375," *Connecticut Explored,* Summer 2014.

Main, Jackson Turner. *Society and Economy in Colonial Connecticut*. Princeton University Press, 1985.

Melish, Joanne Pope. *Disowning Slavery: Gradual Emancipation and "Race" in New England, 1780 – 1860*. Cornell University Press, 1998.

Menschel, David. "Abolition Without Deliverance: The Law of Connecticut Slavery 1784-1848," *Yale Law Journal,* Vol. 111, Issue 1, 2001, http://digitalcommons.law.yale.edu/ylj/vol111/iss1/4.

Murphy, Sharon Ann. *Early American Republic*. Johns Hopkins University Press, 2017.

Oberg, Michael LeRoy. *Uncas: First of the Mohegans*. Cornell University Press, 2006.

Occom, Samson, Joanna Brooks, ed. *The Collected Writings of Samson Occom: Leadership and Literature in Eighteenth Century Native America, Mohegan*. Oxford University Press, 2006.

Pierson, William D., *Black Yankees: The Development of an Afro-American Subculture in Eighteenth-Century New England,* University of Massachusetts Press, 1988.

Shorto, Russell. "On Slavery's Doorstep in Ghana," *The New York Times*, January 30, 2015. https://www.nytimes.com/2015/02/01/travel on-slaverys-doorstep-in-ghana.html.

Steenburg, Nancy and Elizabeth Kading. "The Venture Adventure," *Wrack Lines 6:1,* accessed at http://media.ctseagrant.uconn.edu/ publications/magazines/wracklines/springsummer06/ventadv.pdf.

Stewart, James Brewer, ed. *Venture Smith and the Business of Slavery and Freedom*. University of Massachusetts Press, 2010.

Steiner, Bernard. *History of Slavery in Connecticut*. Johns Hopkins University Press, 1893, https://archive.org/details/historyofslavery00stei.

Sweet, John Wood. *Bodies Politic: Negotiating Race in North America, 1730 – 1830*. University of Pennsylvania Press, 2007.

Vida, Christina. "Nancy Toney's Lifetime in Slavery," *Connecticut Explored*, Winter 2012/2013.

White, David O. *Connecticut's Black Soldiers, 1775 – 1783*. The Pequot Press, 1973.

Descendants of Venture and Marget Smith
at Venture Smith Day, East Haddam, 2018.

Photo: Elizabeth J. Normen

Learn about colonial Connecticut and the southern
New England maritime economy through the words of

Venture Smith

In this true story of freedom, first published in 1798,
Venture Smith tells readers about his capture as a boy
in West Africa, survival of the Middle Passage,
and dramatic quest to free himself from slavery to
become a successful farmer, fisherman, and trader
in the American Revolutionary era.

Recommended for grades 5 – 8

Find curriculum and other resources at
VentureSmithColonialCT.org

LOOK FOR OUR OTHER CONNECTICUT SOCIAL STUDIES RESOURCES, INCLUDING
Where I Live: Connecticut, recommended for grades 3 – 4
WhereILiveCT.org

Connecticut Explored, the magazine of Connecticut history,
recommended for middle and high school and above
CTExplored.org   CTExplored.org/Teach

$10.00
ISBN 978-0-578-55062-6

9 780578 550626